2 KINGS
FROM START2FINISH

MICHAEL WHITWORTH

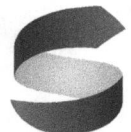

© 2025 by Start2Finish

All rights reserved. No part of this publication may be reproduced, stored in a retrieval system, or transmitted in any form or by any means without the prior written permission of the author. The only exception is brief quotations in printed reviews.

ISBN 978-1-941972-43-4

Published by Start2Finish
Bend, Oregon 97702
start2finish.org

Printed in the United States of America

Unless otherwise noted, all Scripture quotations are from The Holy Bible, English Standard Version®, copyright © 2001 by Crossway Bibles, a publishing ministry of Good News Publishers. Used by permission. All rights reserved.

Cover Design: Evangela Creative

CONTENTS

1.	The Passing of the Mantle	5
2.	Power in Compassion	13
3.	Washed & Made Whole	21
4.	Sight & Salvation	29
5.	Jehu & Judgment	37
6.	Preservation & Promise	45
7.	Mercy in the Midst	53
8.	The Fall of the North	61
9.	Faith Under Siege	69
10.	Faith & Frailty	77
11.	The Book & the King	85
12.	The Fall of Judah	93

1

THE PASSING OF THE MANTLE
2 KINGS 1–2

Objective: To show that God's sovereign work continues through humble servants who trust and obey his word.

INTRODUCTION

Few moments are harder than watching a faithful leader step away. Whether it's a beloved teacher retiring or a parent passing responsibilities to grown children, we feel the weight of transition. Something in us fears that when the mentor departs, the mission might fade.

Israel faced that fear when Elijah's time on earth ended. For years, he had stood as God's lone voice against kings, idols, and drought. Through him, fire fell from heaven, widows were fed, and the nation glimpsed the power of the living God. But now his ministry neared its close, and his disciple Elisha would soon stand alone. Could the work survive when the prophet was gone?

Second Kings 1–2 answers with a resounding "yes." The Lord who judged Ahaziah, sent fire, and parted rivers was not bound to one generation or one man. His word still ruled. His Spirit still moved. The mantle might change shoulders, but the mission did not change hands.

Every Christian community faces the same truth: people come and go, but God's purpose endures. This lesson traces how the Lord affirmed his sovereignty, transferred his power, and renewed his presence through Elisha—the next servant called to carry the flame.

EXAMINATION

Ahaziah's inquiry (1:1–8)

The story of 2 Kings opens where 1 Kings left off—with Ahab's family still on Israel's throne and his spiritual legacy still poisoning the nation. Ahab's son Ahaziah reigns only briefly, but his life perfectly illustrates the decay that idolatry always produces. As soon as his father died, the text reports that "Moab rebelled against Israel" (1:1). Political instability mirrored spiritual rebellion. When a nation turns from God, foreign threats are never far behind.

Soon afterward, Ahaziah suffered a humiliating accident: he fell through the lattice of his upper room in Samaria. Instead of seeking the Lord, he sent messengers to the Philistine city of Ekron to consult Baal-zebub, "the god of flies" (v. 2). The king of Israel—descendant of Abraham, covenant partner of Yahweh—now turned to a pagan idol for healing. Elijah confronted this blasphemy with the piercing question that frames the entire chapter: "Is it because there is no God in Israel that you are going off to consult Baal-zebub, the god of Ekron?" (v. 3).

The prophet's message was not primarily about Ahaziah's health but about Israel's heart. When people look anywhere but to God for guidance, they declare by their actions that he is absent or insufficient. Ahaziah's sin was not ignorance but defiance. He knew Israel's history; he knew the Lord's power. Yet he refused to acknowledge it. His inquiry to a false god was therefore not superstition—it was rebellion.

This moment repeats the great theological issue of 1 Kings 17–22: who truly rules life and death? In Elijah's earlier ministry, God proved himself sovereign over drought, rain, fire, and resurrection. Ahaziah's decision to seek Baal's counsel reopens the very contest that Elijah had already settled on Mount Carmel. The king's fall through the lattice became a physical parable: Israel itself was falling, its structure weakened by the rot of idolatry.

When the messengers returned with Elijah's prophecy, Ahaziah immediately recognized the prophet's description—a hairy man wearing a leather belt (v. 8). The identification carried irony. The king sought a false baal ("lord"), but he encountered instead the true "lord of hair"—Elijah, the genuine servant of the living God. The sovereign Lord would not allow his prophet's word to be mocked or his covenant to be ignored. Ahaziah had invited judgment, and it was already on its way.

Fire from heaven (1:9–18)

Rather than repent, Ahaziah sent a detachment of fifty soldiers to arrest Elijah. The same king who trembled on his sickbed still imagined he could command the prophet of God. The captain ordered, "Man of God, the king says, 'Come down!'" Elijah replied, "If I am a man of God, may fire come down from heaven and consume you and your fifty men" (v. 10). Fire fell, and they perished.

Ahaziah's arrogance persisted. A second captain came with identical words and met the same fiery fate. Only the third captain approached differently: he knelt before Elijah and pleaded for mercy (vv. 13–14). His humility becomes the hinge of the story. The angel of the Lord told Elijah, "Go down with him; do not be afraid of him." The prophet obeyed, descending from the mountain to deliver God's final verdict: "You will not leave the bed you are lying on. You will certainly die" (v. 16).

These episodes recall the confrontation on Mount Carmel. Once again fire from heaven testified that "the Lord, he is God." In a world of rival powers, Elijah's God alone answered by fire. The difference now was the audience: on Carmel, Israel watched; here, a defiant king and his soldiers witnessed the consuming holiness of God.

This narrative highlights the futility of royal authority when it opposes divine authority. Kings may issue commands, but prophets speak the word that shapes reality. The repeated "go up" and "come down" phrases weave a theological irony: Ahaziah, who "fell" from his upper chamber, repeatedly ordered Elijah to "come down," yet it is fire that comes down instead. Pride brings literal and spiritual descent.

The third captain's reverence models the only proper human response to divine power—submission. His plea for life contrasts sharply with his predecessors' arrogance. God's fire is not indiscriminate wrath; it distinguishes between the proud and the humble. When Elijah finally stood before the dying king, he delivered one more message of mercy disguised as judgment. Ahaziah could have repented, as his father briefly did after Naboth's vineyard. Instead, he died "according to the word of the Lord that Elijah had spoken" (v. 17).

Elijah's final confrontation taught Israel that God's word is irresistible. No ladder is tall enough to climb above it, and no guard is strong enough to silence it. The prophet stood alone against royal power, yet heaven itself stood with him. His ministry closes as it began—with fire, faith, and the fierce insistence that there is indeed a God in Israel.

Elijah's departure (2:1–12)

Elijah's life ended as dramatically as it began. From the moment he strode into Ahab's palace to announce drought, he had been the firebrand of Israel—unbending, unpredictable, and utterly devoted to the living God. Yet 2 Kings 2 is not simply the tale of a prophet's exit; it is the assurance that God's work never ends when a servant's task is complete.

The narrator begins, "When the Lord was about to take Elijah up to heaven by a whirlwind…" (v. 1). Elijah knew the end was near, and so did Elisha. Three times Elijah urged his disciple to stay behind—at Gilgal, Bethel, and Jericho—but each time Elisha replied, "As the Lord lives and as you yourself live, I will not leave you." His determination recalls Ruth's vow to Naomi: steadfast love refused to turn back. The prophet's road—from Gilgal to Bethel to Jericho to the Jordan—traced Israel's earliest conquest in reverse. Elijah was retracing the nation's steps as if symbolically withdrawing God's presence from a faithless land. Yet the journey also prepared for renewal, just as Moses once crossed the Red Sea and Joshua the Jordan.

At the Jordan, Elijah rolled up his mantle and struck the water. It divided, and the two men crossed on dry ground. The miracle signaled that the same God who parted seas for Moses still ruled Israel's boundaries. When Elijah asked what gift he might leave behind, Elisha's request was remarkable: "Please let there be a double portion of your spirit on me." In Israelite inheritance law, the eldest son received a "double portion" of his father's estate (Deut. 21:17). Elisha was not asking for twice the power but for rightful succession. He wanted to be Elijah's spiritual heir—the firstborn of the prophetic household.

The request was granted conditionally: "If you see me as I am being taken from you, it shall be so." Moments later, chariots and horses of fire appeared, separating the two men. Elijah ascended in a whirlwind, and Elisha cried, "My father, my father! The chariots of Israel and its horsemen!" (v. 12). The imagery joined heaven and earth in a blaze of glory. Israel's real defense was not its army but its prophets—their prayers, their obedience, their word from God. Elijah's ascension foreshadowed Christ's own: the prophet who "went up" made room for a successor who would carry the Spirit's double share. God's power was not lost; it was multiplied.

Elijah's story ends not with death but translation. Fire once consumed his offerings and his enemies; now it became his chariot home. He departed as he lived—borne by flame, trusting the God who rules storm and sky. His absence, however, did not mean God's silence. A new voice was waiting by the riverbank.

Elisha's first miracles (2:13-25)

When the whirlwind faded, Elisha stood alone, holding his mentor's fallen cloak. The mantle was more than a garment; it was a sign of calling (1 Kgs 19:19). Elisha took it, struck the Jordan, and asked, "Where is the Lord, the God of Elijah?" (v. 14). The river parted again. The answer was clear: Elijah may have been gone, but the Lord remained.

The company of prophets watching from Jericho recognized this immediately: "The spirit of Elijah rests on Elisha." They bowed before him, acknowledging God's transfer of authority. Still, they pleaded to search for Elijah's body, as though unwilling to believe what they had witnessed. They searched three days and found nothing—a faint echo of another three-day search that would one day end with an empty tomb.

Elisha's next act occurred in Jericho, a city once cursed after Joshua's conquest (Josh. 6:26). Its water supply was foul, making the land barren. The people pleaded for help, and Elisha responded with symbolic ritual: he threw salt into the spring, declaring, "Thus says the Lord, 'I have healed this water; from now on neither death nor miscarriage shall come from it.'" The salt signified covenant renewal (Lev. 2:13), not magic. The healing demonstrated that the God who parted the river also restored fertility to a cursed land. Where Elijah's ministry often judged, Elisha's began by blessing. The same power that calls down fire can also bring forth life.

But the prophet's mercy did not dismiss disrespect. As Elisha traveled to Bethel, a group of youths came out to mock him, shouting, "Go up, you baldhead!" (v. 23). Their taunt likely mocked both his prophetic calling and Elijah's ascension—"Go up like your master if you can!" It was open contempt for the Lord's messenger. Elisha cursed them in the Lord's name, and two bears came from the woods, mauling forty-two of the mockers. The story jars modern readers, but in context it reveals that contempt for God's word is never harmless. This episode parallels the fate of Ahaziah's captains: both narratives distinguish between defiance and reverence toward God's servant. Elisha's bears function as covenant enforcers, fulfilling the warnings of Leviticus 26:21–22 that beasts would punish a rebellious people.

Elisha then continued to Mount Carmel and Samaria—the same regions where Elijah once contended with Baal and confronted kings. The circle was complete: the Lord had not abandoned Israel. The Spirit rested on a new servant, and the prophetic torch had passed. Elijah's fiery zeal was now joined with Elisha's restorative grace. Judgment and mercy remain twin flames of the same divine presence.

From this point forward, Elisha would become God's primary voice in Israel, confronting rulers, aiding widows, feeding the hungry, and healing the nations. The Lord had again proven faithful to his covenant promise: he would never leave his people without a prophet, without a word, and without hope.

APPLICATION

1. God alone deserves our trust

Ahaziah's greatest sin was not his fall but where he turned for help afterward. He knew Israel's history, yet he sought answers from Ekron instead of from heaven. Many Christians repeat the same folly—trusting human wisdom, political strength, or personal control more than God's word. Scripture asks the same question Elijah posed: "Is there no God in Israel?" (1:3). Every crisis becomes a test of trust. We cannot serve the Lord and still consult modern idols for direction. When fear tempts us to seek easier assurances, faith must answer that God remains enough. Healing, provision, and guidance belong to him alone.

2. Humility preserves what pride destroys

The two captains who demanded Elijah "come down" were consumed by fire; the third, who knelt in humility, was spared. The difference was not in rank but in reverence. Pride assumes God's power can be managed; humility recognizes that it can only be received. The story teaches that submission is safety. When we approach God on our knees rather than on our terms, judgment turns to mercy. The Lord resists the proud but gives grace to the humble. In every age, obedience and humility remain the only path to life.

3. God's work never ends with one servant

Elijah's departure could have signaled the end of prophetic guidance, yet his mantle fell upon Elisha. God's mission never depends on a single messenger. When one laborer's time is done, another rises to continue the work. Churches often fear transition, but 2 Kings 2 reminds us that leadership changes are part of God's design, not signs of his absence. The Spirit who empowered Elijah empowered Elisha. The same Lord still equips new servants to proclaim his word. Our task is to be faithful where we stand and to train others who will carry the mantle forward when our work is complete.

4. Reverence for God's word brings renewal

Elisha's miracles reveal that the word of God both heals and warns. Jericho's water became pure because the prophet obeyed God's command; Bethel's mockers suffered because they despised it. The same word that restores life also confronts sin. Renewal in the church depends on our willingness to honor Scripture as holy ground. We must approach worship, doctrine, and daily obedience with the reverence Elisha demanded. God's word is not casual advice but covenant truth. Those who honor it find healing waters; those who mock it drink only bitterness.

CONCLUSION

The opening chapters of 2 Kings remind us that God's faithfulness outlives every generation. A king's arrogance could not silence his word, and a prophet's departure could not end his work. Fire fell, waters parted, and a new servant rose to carry the mantle. The same Lord still reigns over his people today.

As the story of 2 Kings turns to Elisha's ministry, we move from succession to service—from the passing of a mantle to the power of mercy. In the next few lessons, Elisha's miracles will reveal how God's compassion reaches widows, soldiers, and nations alike. The prophet who crossed the Jordan now brings living water to a thirsty world.

REFLECTION

1. Why did Ahaziah's inquiry of Baal-zebub expose Israel's deeper spiritual condition?

2. What does Elijah's question, "Is there no God in Israel?" reveal about true faith?

3. How does the third captain's humility illustrate the right response to God's authority?

4. Why did Elisha ask for a "double portion" of Elijah's spirit?

5. What lessons about God's character appear in the miracles at the Jordan and Jericho?

6. How does Elisha's response to the mockers at Bethel show reverence for God's word?

DISCUSSION

1. What modern "Baal-zebubs" tempt Christians to seek help apart from God?

2. How can humility protect us from the pride that destroys faith?

3. What attitudes help churches handle leadership transitions with faith instead of fear?

4. In what ways can we "pick up the mantle" of older Christians today?

5. How does reverence for God's word bring healing to a congregation or home?

6. Where do you most need to trust that God's work continues beyond your control?

2

POWER IN COMPASSION
2 KINGS 3-4

Objective: To demonstrate that God's power is revealed through compassion that restores, provides, and gives life.

INTRODUCTION

Some people show their strength by how loudly they speak; others by how gently they serve. The truest kind of power, however, is not measured in noise or display—it is power that heals, restores, and provides.

After Elijah's whirlwind departure, many in Israel must have wondered whether the fire had gone out with him. He had been the man of judgment—the prophet who called down flames from heaven and silenced false gods. His successor, Elisha, inherited that same Spirit, yet his ministry took a different tone. The thunder became a whisper. Judgment gave way to mercy. God's power now moved through compassion.

In 2 Kings 3-4, the miracles of Elisha show that the Lord's might is not limited to mountains and thrones. He fills trenches for thirsty armies, multiplies oil for widows, raises sons for grieving mothers, and turns famine into feast for hungry prophets. Each story reveals the same truth: divine compassion is not weakness but strength in service of love.

This lesson invites Christians to see God's power not only in acts of justice but also in moments of mercy. When provision comes quietly, life is restored tenderly, and faith grows through kindness. The God who once sent fire now pours out grace through his servant's gentle hands.

EXAMINATION

War with Moab (3:1–27)

After Elijah's ascension, the spotlight turns to Elisha. His ministry began not on a mountaintop of fire but in the muddy valleys of human need. The first test arrived through politics. Moab, long subdued since David's reign, rebelled against Israel after Ahab's death (3:5). King Jehoram, Ahab's son, joined forces with Jehoshaphat of Judah and the king of Edom to suppress the revolt. What began as a show of military strength quickly became a journey into dependence on God.

The coalition marched through the wilderness of Edom, only to run out of water after seven days. Their power dried up as fast as the desert sand. Panic spread until Jehoshaphat remembered there was a prophet nearby—Elisha, the servant of Elijah. Once again Judah's faith had to steady Israel's unbelief.

Elisha's reception of Jehoram was frosty: "What have I to do with you? Go to the prophets of your father and of your mother" (v. 13). The prophet would act only for Jehoshaphat's sake. The scene echoes Elijah before Ahab: truth still bowed to no throne. Yet even in judgment, mercy found a path. Elisha called for a musician, and as music filled the camp, the hand of the Lord came upon him. He prophesied that God would fill the valley with water—without wind, without rain—enough for the army and their animals (vv. 16–17).

At dawn the prophecy was fulfilled. Water miraculously flowed from Edom, pooling across the valley floor. From Moab's vantage point, the red reflection of sunrise on the water looked like blood. Believing their enemies had slaughtered one another, the Moabites rushed in to plunder—and ran straight into an ambush. Israel and her allies won decisively.

The victory, however, ended with darkness. The king of Moab, driven to desperation, sacrificed his firstborn son on the city wall (v. 27). The text says, "There came great wrath against Israel, and they withdrew." Scholars differ on whose wrath this was—Moab's, Israel's, or God's—but the moral shock is unmistakable.

This episode teaches that miracles of provision can accompany people who still lack submission. God gave water because of his faithfulness, not because of Israel's righteousness. The desert pools testified that his mercy sustains even faltering faith, yet the blood-soaked wall warns that unbelief always leads back to despair.

The widow's oil (4:1–7)

If chapter 3 shows God's compassion for kings and nations, chapter 4 turns to a nameless widow. Her husband, one of the "sons of the prophets," had died, and creditors threatened to take her two sons as slaves. The widow cried out, and Elisha asked, "What shall I do for you? Tell me, what have you in the house?" (v. 2). Her answer—"nothing…except a jar of oil"—became the seed of provision. The prophet instructed her to borrow as many empty vessels as she could, then to shut the door and pour. As she obeyed, the oil flowed until every container was full. Only when she said, "There is not another," did the flow stop (v. 6). She sold the oil, paid her debts, and lived on the remainder.

The miracle's simplicity conceals profound theology. God multiplied what the widow already possessed; grace began with faith's small offering. Her obedience, privacy, and trust stand in contrast to Ahaziah's defiance and Jehoram's hesitation. The same Lord who filled desert trenches with water now filled kitchen jars with oil.

The Shunammite woman (4:8–37)

The next scene shifts from poverty to prosperity, but the same God is present in both. A "wealthy woman" in Shunem regularly provided food and lodging for Elisha as he traveled. Recognizing her generosity, the prophet asked what could be done for her. She sought no political favor or royal audience—her only desire was contentment. Gehazi, Elisha's servant, noticed that she had no child, and Elisha promised that she would bear a son within a year (v. 16). The word of the Lord again brought life where none existed.

Years later tragedy struck. The promised child suddenly collapsed in the field and died in his mother's arms. Her response was one of determined faith: she saddled a donkey and rode to Mount Carmel, refusing delay. When she reached Elisha, she fell at his feet and cried, "Did I ask my lord for a son? Did I not say, 'Do not deceive me'?" (v. 28). Her grief was raw, but her hope was fierce—she went directly to God's prophet, not away from him.

Elisha first sent Gehazi with his staff to lay upon the boy, but nothing happened. Only when Elisha himself entered the room did life return. He prayed, stretched himself over the child, and the boy sneezed seven times before opening his eyes (v. 35). The miracle recalled Elijah's raising of the widow's son at Zarephath (1 Kgs. 17:17-24), yet this one is more intimate. The prophet's own body became the conduit of divine breath.

Some have called this episode the centerpiece of Elisha's ministry because it combined faith, intercession, and resurrection. The woman's faith refused to surrender even when all visible hope was gone. Elisha's persistence showed that God's compassion is personal, not mechanical; he does not delegate life—he gives it. The seven sneezes symbolized the fullness of restoration: what sin and death destroyed, the Spirit renewed. The same God who can send fire and water can also give life where there was none.

The Shunammite woman stands as one of Scripture's most vivid pictures of active faith. She did not treat the prophet's promise as sentimental comfort but as covenant truth. Her story invites all believers to approach God with the same mixture of reverence and boldness. She asked for no sign, yet she receives resurrection.

Death in the pot and bread for a hundred (4:38-44)

The chapter closes with two brief miracles that display God's care for his prophets during famine. In the first, Elisha returned to Gilgal where a company of prophets faced hunger. While stew was being prepared, one of them accidentally added wild gourds—poisonous fruit. The men cried out, "O man of God, there is death in the pot!" (v. 40). Elisha calmly added flour to the stew and declared it safe. The danger was neutralized, and the meal became nourishment.

The narrative may seem small beside chariots of fire, yet its symbolism is rich. The poisoned pot represented the corruption of Israel's spiritual life; Elisha's act foreshadowed the healing power of God's word to purify what sin has spoiled. The flour had no chemical power—it was an act of faith.

Immediately afterward another need arose. A man from Baal-shalishah brought twenty barley loaves and fresh grain for the prophets. Elisha commanded that it be set before one hundred men. Gehazi protested, "How can I set this before a hundred men?" (v. 43). But the prophet replied, "Thus says the Lord, 'They shall eat and have some left.'" The food was distributed, and "they ate and had some left, according to the word of the Lord."

This final scene intentionally echoes later in the gospels. Jesus would multiply loaves and fish for multitudes, fulfilling what Elisha prefigured. Both miracles declare the same truth: God provides abundantly for those who serve him. His word creates sufficiency in scarcity. The prophetic community—small, hungry, and faithful—experienced firsthand the sustaining mercy of God.

The progression of these stories is striking. Chapter 3 revealed God's power in public warfare; chapter 4 showed that the same power dwells in quiet households and humble kitchens. Through Elisha, divine strength took on a gentler face. Compassion became the new expression of conquest. The God who conquered Baal now conquered despair.

APPLICATION

1. God provides even when faith falters

Israel's campaign against Moab was an act of politics more than piety, yet God still sent water. Jehoram had inherited his parents' idols and hardly deserved divine favor, but the Lord honored Jehoshaphat's faith and his own covenant mercy. Grace does not wait for spotless faith before acting. Even when our motives are mixed, God can turn dry valleys into pools of refreshment. The soldiers still had to dig trenches—faith does not remove effort—but God filled them with unexpected abundance. When the sun rose, what looked like failure became victory. Christians today often face deserts of exhaustion or doubt, but this story assures us that God's compassion is deeper than our shortcomings. He supplies strength when obedience seems small and brings living water where we see only dust.

2. God multiplies what we offer in faith

The widow's story teaches that divine power often begins with ordinary obedience. She had nothing left but a small jar of oil, yet that meager possession became the vessel of a miracle. Elisha did not hand her riches; he required trust. She borrowed jars, shut the door, and poured until there were no containers left. God still multiplies what we surrender to him. Faith opens the spout; fear closes it. Each act of trust—whether giving generously, serving quietly, or praying persistently—becomes a jar that God can fill. The miracle reminds Christians that scarcity is not a barrier to grace but the setting where grace shines brightest. When we bring our "nothing but a jar," God fills it beyond measure, providing both provision for the moment and hope for tomorrow.

3. God's compassion extends to every condition

Elisha ministered to widows and wealthy women, to soldiers and starving prophets. Compassion was not an interruption in his ministry—it was the ministry itself. The Shunammite woman stands as proof that God's care reaches beyond social rank or circumstance. Whether in a humble kitchen or a furnished upper room, the same Lord listens and responds. In her story, grief met resurrection; faith met fulfillment. Elisha's touch anticipated the tenderness of Christ, who raised sons and fed multitudes centuries later. Christians are called to embody mercy: to notice the hurting, to comfort the weary, and to celebrate with those restored. Compassion is not weakness; it is divine strength expressed through gentleness. When the church mirrors Elisha's kindness, the world sees the living heart of God.

4. God's word brings life to what is poisoned

The prophets' stew at Gilgal was ruined by ignorance, but the Lord turned danger into nourishment through a word and a handful of flour. The act was symbolic—truth healing corruption. In every age, spiritual poison threatens God's people: false doctrine, cynicism, bitterness, and fear. Only the pure word of God can restore health to a tainted soul or congregation. Likewise, the multiplication of bread shows that obedience to God's word creates abundance where reason expects lack. When we trust his commands, he not only removes what kills but also multiplies what sustains. Churches today must keep adding the flour of truth to the world's poisoned pot—teaching sound doctrine, modeling holiness, and trusting that God's power still turns famine into feast. Where his word is honored, life always follows.

CONCLUSION

Through Elisha, God displayed power wrapped in mercy. He supplied water to armies, oil to widows, life to a child, and food to prophets. Each act showed that the Lord's strength is never cold or distant—it always moves toward the hurting. The God who rules nations also fills jars and heals hearts.

As the story continues, that compassion will extend beyond Israel's borders. In the next lesson, a foreign commander named Naaman will discover that the same God who helps widows and prophets also cleanses outsiders. The Lord who heals poisoned stews will soon heal a leper's skin—and a proud man's soul.

REFLECTION

1. Why did Elisha refuse to help Jehoram except for Jehoshaphat's sake?
2. What does God's provision of water in the desert reveal about his mercy?
3. How did the widow's obedience demonstrate her faith in God's power?
4. What stands out about the Shunammite woman's persistence and trust in Elisha's word?
5. How do Elisha's miracles show God's compassion toward both the rich and the poor?
6. What do the flour and loaves symbolize about God's ability to purify and provide?

DISCUSSION

1. How has God provided for you even when your faith was weak?
2. What small act of obedience might God be waiting to multiply in your life?
3. How can we show compassion that reflects God's heart in everyday settings?
4. Why is compassion a sign of strength, not weakness, in Christian service?
5. What are some "poisons" that threaten the church today, and how can truth heal them?
6. How can your congregation become a place where God's word turns scarcity into abundance?

3

WASHED & MADE WHOLE
2 KINGS 5

Objective: To show that God's grace cleanses the humble and condemns the proud who abuse it.

INTRODUCTION

Some lessons in life come wrapped in mud. A young child falls into a puddle, covered from head to toe, and rushes inside in tears. A parent doesn't scold but smiles, knowing that sometimes the best stories begin when pride gets dirty. In 2 Kings 5, a powerful man learned that same truth from the banks of the Jordan River.

Naaman was a hero in Syria, a soldier with medals, victories, and the respect of kings. But beneath his armor hid the shame of leprosy—a sickness that no power could cure. When an Israelite slave girl whispered that healing could be found through a prophet in Samaria, the general began a journey that would wash away more than disease.

Elisha offered no ceremony, no spectacle—only a command: "Go and wash in the Jordan seven times." Pride protested; obedience prevailed. Naaman emerged from the water not only clean but also changed. The man who came to buy a miracle left confessing the one true God.

This lesson explores how God's grace crosses boundaries, how humility opens the door to healing, and how greed can destroy what gratitude preserves. The river still runs clear for every soul willing to step down into its mercy.

EXAMINATION

Naaman's condition (5:1-7)

The story opens far from Israel's borders. Naaman, the commander of the Aramean army, stands as one of Scripture's most surprising seekers. He was a Gentile general, victorious in battle and favored by his king, yet his victories couldn't hide his affliction: "He was a mighty man of valor, but he was a leper" (v. 1). That single clause—"but he was a leper"—undoes every human boast. Power, rank, and reputation crumble before the frailty of the flesh.

Leprosy in the ancient world was more than a disease; it was a stigma. It separated a man from others and from worship. For Naaman, whose identity was wrapped in command and prestige, leprosy exposed the limits of strength. His need prepared him for grace. God's compassion begins its work where human ability ends.

Into this unlikely setting enters a young Israelite girl, taken captive during an Aramean raid. Though enslaved, she spoke with faith and mercy: "Would that my lord were with the prophet who is in Samaria! He would cure him of his leprosy" (v. 3). Her quiet witness became the hinge of redemption. She did not curse her captor; she pointed him toward healing. The might of a nation depended on the faith of a child.

Naaman carried her report to his king, who sent him to Israel with lavish gifts—silver, gold, and garments. Political pomp replaced humble faith. When Naaman arrived with a royal letter, Israel's king panicked: "Am I God, to kill and to make alive?" (v. 7). He tore his clothes, assuming the request was a provocation for war. The contrast is deliberate. The pagan general sought mercy; the covenant king forgot it existed. Israel's king had prophets but no trust, while a foreign soldier journeyed in hope.

This irony reveals Israel's spiritual anemia. Those who should proclaim God's power doubted it; those who had no covenant came seeking it. God's grace often travels along unexpected roads—sometimes through conquered servants, sometimes through fearful kings—to reach those willing to listen.

The prophet's command (5:8–14)

Elisha steps into the story as the calm voice of divine purpose. Hearing that the king had torn his garments, the prophet sent word: "Let him come to me, that he may know that there is a prophet in Israel" (v. 8). The prophet's confidence contrasts the king's despair. God still worked in Israel, though faith was scarce at court.

Naaman arrived at Elisha's house with his chariots and horses—symbols of power rolling into the modest home of a man who owns none. But Elisha did not even come out to meet him. Instead, he sent a messenger: "Go and wash in the Jordan seven times, and your flesh shall be restored, and you shall be clean" (v. 10).

The simplicity of the command offended Naaman. "Behold, I thought that he would surely come out to me... and call upon the name of the Lord his God" (v. 11). Pride resents grace when it arrives without ceremony. He wanted spectacle; God required submission. Naaman's protest echoes every heart that wishes to be healed without humility. The Jordan, muddy and unimpressive compared to Damascus's rivers, became the dividing line between arrogance and obedience.

Naaman turned away in rage, but his servants pleaded with him to reconsider: "My father, it is a great word the prophet has spoken to you; will you not do it?" (v. 13). Their reasoning was gentle and wise. They reminded him that faith is rarely complicated; it is simply hard to surrender. Their appeal mirrors the captive girl's earlier faith—humble voices leading a proud man to obedience.

At last Naaman went down to the Jordan and dipped himself seven times. The number seven, signifying completeness, marked the perfection of God's work. When he rose, "his flesh was restored like the flesh of a little child, and he was clean" (v. 14). The mighty warrior became childlike both in skin and in spirit. He entered Israel as a conqueror; he emerged as a convert.

The cleansing prefigured salvation itself: healing that comes through trust, not transaction. God's grace flows through word, water, and obedience—the same pattern that echoes through the gospel call to repentance and baptism. Pride resists such simplicity, but those who submit find restoration deeper than flesh.

Grace for a Gentile (5:15-19)

Naaman returned to Elisha a changed man. The text emphasizes not only his healed skin but also his transformed heart: "Behold, I know that there is no God in all the earth but in Israel" (v. 15). What began as a search for a physical cure became a confession of faith. The commander, who once demanded attention, now stood before the prophet in gratitude. His first instinct was to offer gifts, but Elisha refused: "As the Lord lives, before whom I stand, I will receive none" (v. 16).

Elisha's refusal served two purposes. First, it protected God's grace from being mistaken as merchandise. Salvation is not a transaction. Second, it distinguished Yahweh from the gods of Aram, whose priests demanded payment. The prophet's stance declared that divine favor cannot be purchased with silver or power.

Still, Naaman's heart sought to respond. He asked to take two muleloads of earth back to Syria so that he might worship the Lord on Israel's soil (v. 17). Though his understanding was limited, his desire was sincere: he wished to honor the God who healed him. He also confessed a tension—his duty to escort the Aramean king into the temple of Rimmon. Naaman pleaded for pardon when forced by duty to bow there. Elisha responded not with legalism but with grace: "Go in peace" (v. 19).

This is not permission for idolatry but recognition of a heart turning toward God within a pagan culture. Naaman's faith would now be tested amid compromise and pressure, as all faith is. Elisha's words anticipate Jesus' later declaration to forgiven sinners: "Go in peace." The cleansing waters of the Jordan foreshadowed the living water of Christ's salvation—a gift that would one day flow beyond Israel to all the nations.

Naaman's story, therefore, is not simply about healing skin but about the widening mercy of God. A Gentile commander received what many in Israel rejected: grace through obedient faith. The same river that symbolized humility became a sign of the gospel's reach. God's compassion crossed borders long before Peter's vision in Acts 10 or Paul's missionary journeys. In Naaman's bath, the nations began to see the heart of Israel's God.

Gehazi's greed (5:20-27)

The chapter closes with a stark contrast. Naaman left rejoicing; Gehazi,

Elisha's servant, left cursed. The story that began with a Gentile healed ends with an Israelite defiled.

Gehazi could not bear to see wealth slip away untaken. He said to himself, "My master has spared this Naaman the Syrian… as the Lord lives, I will run after him and get something from him" (v. 20). The phrase "as the Lord lives"—so often a mark of prophetic truth—became an oath of deceit. Gehazi ran, lied, and received from Naaman silver and garments. The healed foreigner now became the generous one; the prophet's servant became the greedy one.

When Gehazi returned, Elisha asked, "Where have you been?"—the same divine question posed to Adam in Eden. Gehazi's denial exposed not only his greed but also his blindness. Elisha replied, "Did not my heart go when the man turned from his chariot to meet you?" (v. 26). The prophet's words pierced deeper than accusation; they exposed spiritual hypocrisy. Gehazi's desire for payment betrayed the purity of God's grace that Elisha had so carefully guarded.

The judgment was swift and symbolic: "Therefore the leprosy of Naaman shall cling to you and to your descendants forever" (v. 27). The disease that had marked an unbelieving Gentile now marked a deceitful Israelite. The roles were reversed—grace had cleansed an outsider, and judgment had fallen on one inside.

Gehazi's punishment parallels Achan's theft from Jericho: in both cases, greed polluted holy victory. Naaman's washing prefigures baptism, while Gehazi's punishment warns that grace can be abused. The same waters that heal can condemn those who twist them for gain.

The narrative offers a sobering reminder: proximity to holy things does not guarantee holiness. Gehazi witnessed miracles but never embraced their message. His leprosy stands as a visible sermon to Israel: God's favor rests not on heritage but on humility.

APPLICATION

1. God's grace reaches beyond every boundary

Naaman's healing reminds us that God's compassion is not confined by geography, race, or reputation. The commander of Israel's enemy army became a recipient of divine mercy because his heart turned toward obedience. God has always welcomed the humble—no matter how far they come or how flawed they are. His grace does not stop at the borders of Israel or any other social circle. The gospel continues that same invitation to the ends of the earth. Christians are called to embody this generosity, refusing to treat anyone as beyond the reach of redemption. The river that cleansed Naaman still flows, offering hope to all who will descend into its waters of trust.

2. Obedience, not pride, opens the way to healing

Naaman's pride nearly cost him his cure. He expected ceremony, not simplicity; grandeur, not humility. Yet the Jordan's muddy current became his path to renewal. God often places blessings behind instructions that seem ordinary or beneath us. Faith is proven not by feeling but by action—by stepping into the water when reason scoffs. Elisha's word to Naaman echoes God's call to every sinner: wash and be clean. When believers humble themselves to obey God's word—especially in commands like baptism, forgiveness, and service—they discover that submission is not humiliation but liberation.

3. Gratitude protects the heart from greed

Elisha refused Naaman's gifts because grace cannot be purchased. Gehazi's downfall proves how easily gratitude can twist into greed. Having seen miracles, he still wanted profit. The moment he tried to own what belonged to God, he lost the purity of his service. Gratitude is content with God's provision; greed always demands more. In a world that markets even spirituality, Christians must remember that salvation is free but never cheap. The proper response to grace is thanksgiving expressed in generosity, not manipulation. A grateful heart gives freely because it knows it has received freely. When we guard gratitude, greed cannot corrupt us.

4. Humble influence can change lives

The most powerful voice in Naaman's story was not a prophet or a king but a captive girl. Her compassion toward her oppressor introduced him to the living God. Faith expressed through kindness can pierce the hardest hearts. Too often Christians underestimate the influence of quiet integrity and gentle testimony. God still uses ordinary people to open doors for extraordinary grace. When believers speak with hope instead of bitterness, they become bridges of healing in a divided world. The gospel spreads when compassion outweighs resentment and when our faith points others, even enemies, toward the One who can make them whole.

CONCLUSION

Naaman's story proves that grace can reach where pride cannot. A soldier's healing, a servant's deceit, and a prophet's steadfast faith reveal both the wideness and seriousness of God's mercy. The same Lord who washed a Gentile clean also judged a greedy Israelite, reminding every generation that grace must never be taken for granted or gain.

As Elisha's ministry continues, God's compassion will stretch even further. In the next lesson, we'll see how that mercy sustained a nation in famine and protected his people in war. The prophet who cleansed a leper would soon open blind eyes and feed the hungry—proof again that God's power is never absent where faith abides.

REFLECTION

1. How does Naaman's leprosy reveal the limits of human strength and achievement?
2. Why is the faith of the captive Israelite girl so significant?
3. What does Naaman's initial anger at Elisha's command teach about pride?
4. How does Naaman's washing in the Jordan illustrate God's grace and obedience?
5. What can we learn from Elisha's refusal to accept Naaman's gifts?
6. Why did Gehazi's greed turn God's gift of grace into judgment?

DISCUSSION

1. What barriers sometimes keep people today from accepting God's grace as Naaman did?
2. How can pride keep us from obeying God's simple commands?
3. In what ways does gratitude protect our hearts from greed and resentment?
4. How can believers reflect God's grace toward those outside their faith community?
5. What lessons can we learn from the captive girl's humble witness?
6. How might our attitudes toward generosity and service reveal our understanding of grace?

4

SIGHT & SALVATION
2 KINGS 6–8

Objective: To show that faith sees God's unseen power working through every danger, detail, and deliverance.

INTRODUCTION

Sometimes the hardest part of faith is learning to see. A young child once stood in a dark room, frightened by shadows dancing on the wall. His father switched on the light, and suddenly the shapes turned out to be nothing more than toys and books—familiar, harmless things. The room hadn't changed; only his eyes had.

In 2 Kings 6–8, Elisha's ministry teaches that faith depends on that same kind of sight. The prophet's servant saw only armies; Elisha saw heaven's chariots. A starving city saw famine; God saw tomorrow's feast. The same power that makes iron float and kingdoms fall also opens eyes to realities invisible to fear.

These chapters weave together small mercies and sweeping miracles—recovering a borrowed tool, feeding enemies, saving cities, and preserving kings. Through every scene, one truth endures: salvation begins when God helps his people see what he sees. When fear blinds, faith must ask, "Lord, open my eyes."

This lesson explores how divine vision reshapes our understanding of danger, deliverance, and destiny. The God who surrounded his prophet with fiery horses still surrounds his people today—with mercy stronger than armies and promises brighter than despair.

EXAMINATION

The floating axe head (6:1-7)

Elisha's ministry opens this section with a miracle so ordinary that it might seem trivial beside wars and healings. Yet the story of the lost axe head reveals that God's compassion extends even to borrowed tools and anxious hearts.

The "sons of the prophets" had outgrown their dwelling near the Jordan and began cutting trees for a new home. In the middle of the work, one man's iron axe head flew into the river. His cry was immediate: "Alas, my master! It was borrowed!" (v. 5). For a poor apprentice, this loss meant shame and unpayable debt.

Elisha's response was calm and simple. He asked where it fell, cut a stick, and threw it into the water, and the iron floated. The man reached out and took it (v. 7). No thunder, no crowd, just quiet restoration.

This episode reminds readers that God is not detached from daily life. The same Lord who parted seas also helped retrieve a borrowed tool. Elisha's miracle sanctified ordinary labor—showing that divine power is not reserved for crises. The stick cast into the river prefigured the cross: wood overturning the laws of nature to bring back what was lost. God's grace redeems the small, the simple, and the submerged.

For the community of prophets, the event confirms that the Spirit of Elijah truly rested on Elisha. Every moment—public or private—belongs to a God who cares. His salvation is not only cosmic but also personal, restoring what sin, neglect, or loss has swallowed.

Chariots of fire and opened eyes (6:8-23)

The next narrative widens the scale from a single axe to an entire army. Aram again waged war against Israel, but each time the king of Aram planned an ambush, Elisha revealed it to Israel's king. God's prophet became the nation's secret defense network. Furious, the Aramean king demanded Elisha's capture and learned he was in Dothan. By night he sent horses, chariots, and troops to surround the city.

When Elisha's servant rose early and saw the enemy encircling them, he panicked: "Alas, my master! What shall we do?" (v. 15). Elisha answered with calm assurance: "Do not be afraid, for those who are with us are more than those who are with them" (v. 16). Then he prayed, "O Lord, please open his eyes that he may see." The servant's eyes were opened, and he beheld the mountain full of horses and chariots of fire all around Elisha (v. 17).

The unseen reality was suddenly visible. Heaven's armies had been present all along; faith, not sight, revealed them. This moment embodies one of the central themes of Kings: God's invisible sovereignty protects his people even when danger appears overwhelming. Elisha did not summon the heavenly host—they were already there. His prayer was not for deliverance but for perception.

When the Arameans advanced, Elisha prayed again, this time for blindness, and they were struck with confusion. He led them into Samaria, where their eyes were opened before Israel's king. The king wanted to kill them, but Elisha forbade it: "Set bread and water before them, that they may eat and drink and go to their master" (v. 22). The enemies who came to destroy were fed instead. Peace followed for a time between Aram and Israel.

Together, these two miracles—the floating axe and the opened eyes—reveal a God equally present in the ordinary and the overwhelming. His salvation rescues the small and disarms the strong, teaching that true sight sees providence where fear sees peril.

The siege of Samaria (6:24–7:20)

Peace with Aram did not last. Ben-hadad returned and besieged Samaria, driving the city into desperation. The famine became so severe that a donkey's head sold for eighty shekels of silver, and mothers resorted to unthinkable acts to survive (6:25-29). The king of Israel, appalled yet unrepentant, blamed Elisha: "May God do so to me and more also, if the head of Elisha remains on his shoulders today" (v. 31). Crisis again exposed misplaced faith—he cursed the prophet instead of repenting to God.

Elisha, however, remained steadfast. He announced a divine reversal: "Tomorrow about this time a seah of fine flour shall be sold for a shekel, and two seahs of barley for a shekel, at the gate of Samaria" (7:1). An officer scoffed, "If the Lord himself should make windows in heaven, could this thing be?" Elisha replied, "You shall see it with your own eyes, but you shall not eat of it" (7:2). Faith divides those who live from those who only look.

That night, God caused the Aramean army to hear the sound of chariots and horses. Believing Israel has hired foreign allies, they fled in panic, leaving their tents, food, and treasure behind. Outside the city, four lepers—outcasts living between despair and death—decided to surrender to the enemy camp. They discovered it deserted and feasted amid abundance. Realizing the good news, they said, "We are not doing right. This day is a day of good news; if we are silent… punishment will overtake us" (7:9). They rushed to tell the city.

At dawn, the prophecy was fulfilled exactly as Elisha said: grain sold cheaply, life returned, and the skeptical officer was trampled in the gate. The proud saw God's salvation but did not taste it. This narrative mirrors the gospel itself—those rejected by society became the first heralds of good news, while the self-assured perished in unbelief. The lepers acted as proto-evangelists: they received grace freely and shared it urgently. God's deliverance transformed famine into feast and shame into proclamation.

This story, perhaps more than any in Elisha's ministry, showcases the rhythm of divine reversal. The invisible became visible, the hungry became full, and the hopeless city survived by grace. Sight without faith leads to death; faith that acts on God's word brings life.

Restoration and revolution (8:1–15)

Chapter 8 opens with another act of restoration. Elisha warned the Shunammite woman—whose son he once raised from the dead—to leave Israel because of an impending seven-year famine. She obeyed and later returned, finding her property confiscated. As she appealed to the king, Gehazi happened to be recounting her earlier miracle. The timing was providential: "Restore all that was hers," ordered the king (v. 6). The woman who once lost her child now received her home and harvest. God's providence wove mercy through obedience and memory.

Immediately after, the tone darkens. Elisha traveled to Damascus and met Hazael, a servant of Ben-hadad. The king, ill, sent Hazael to inquire whether he would recover. Elisha replied, "Say to him, 'You shall certainly recover,' but the Lord has shown me that he shall certainly die" (v. 10).

The prophet then wept, foreseeing the cruelty Hazael would inflict upon Israel—burning fortresses, killing the young, and dashing infants (v. 12). Hazael feigned surprise but soon returned and smothered his master, seizing the throne.

These final vignettes in Elisha's ministry illustrate both restoration and revolution—God reinstating the faithful and reshaping nations through means that defy human control. The Shunammite's homecoming demonstrates personal grace; Hazael's coronation warns that divine justice may arrive through uncomfortable instruments. Through both mercy and judgment, God's hand remains steady.

Decline in Judah (8:16–29)

While Elisha continued his prophetic work in Israel, the southern kingdom of Judah began to follow the same dark path. Jehoram son of Jehoshaphat inherited a stable throne and a godly heritage, yet he squandered both. Scripture says, "He walked in the way of the kings of Israel, as the house of Ahab had done, for the daughter of Ahab was his wife" (v. 18). By marrying Athaliah, Ahab's daughter, Jehoram imported idolatry into Judah's palace. The alliance that once seemed politically wise became spiritually ruinous.

His reign was marked by rebellion and loss. Edom and Libnah broke away, shrinking Judah's borders (vv. 20–22). The narrator explains that these defeats were not random—they were the Lord's response to covenant infidelity. Yet, in mercy, "the Lord was not willing to destroy Judah, for the sake of David his servant" (v. 19). God's promise to preserve David's line restrained total collapse. Even in judgment, grace held a remnant.

After Jehoram's death, his son Ahaziah reigned briefly. Influenced by his mother, Athaliah, and her northern kin, he "walked in the way of the house of Ahab" (v. 27). His partnership with Joram of Israel in battle against Hazael of Aram set the stage for the bloody purges that would soon follow. Both kings were wounded at Ramoth-gilead, and their intertwined fates would culminate in Jehu's revolution (chs. 9–10). Still, through the smoke of rebellion, God's covenant mercy continued. The lamp of David flickered but did not go out.

APPLICATION

1. God cares about the smallest troubles

The floating axe head proves that divine concern reaches into ordinary places. The same Lord who commands armies also restores what seems insignificant. Many Christians assume God is too grand to notice their daily frustrations, yet Elisha's quiet miracle contradicts that fear. God's grace sanctifies every life detail. When we invite him into the workshop and the kitchen, not just into worship, we discover that every loss matters to him. Nothing is too small for prayer or too common for providence. Faith learns to see the sacred in the simple—because a God who can make iron float can certainly bear the weight of our burdens.

2. Faith opens eyes when fear blinds

Elisha's servant saw only enemy horses; the prophet saw fiery ones from heaven. Fear limits sight to what surrounds us, but faith sees who surrounds our fear. God rarely removes threats before revealing himself within them. Spiritual vision requires trust that the unseen world is no less real than the visible one. In every crisis, believers must pray, "Lord, open my eyes." When God grants that vision, courage replaces panic, and mercy replaces vengeance. The same power that blinded Aram also enlightened Elisha's servant—proof that sight depends not on circumstance but on surrender. The eyes of faith discern invisible help, and those who see God's armies need never fear man's.

3. God turns despair into deliverance

Samaria's siege exposed human helplessness and divine sufficiency. A starving city became a banquet overnight, and four lepers became the first preachers of good news. God delights to reverse expectations—to make the outcast the messenger, the hopeless the herald. When faith seems scarce, hope still waits at the gate. The story urges Christians to trust that no famine is final, no darkness too deep for God's dawn. His word can transform scarcity into surplus within a single day. Yet it also warns that unbelief forfeits the feast. The skeptical officer saw but never tasted because he doubted the promise. Faith acts on God's word even when reason cannot imagine how it will come true.

4. God's promise outlasts corruption

The closing scenes remind us that divine faithfulness persists even when kings fail. Judah's decline under Jehoram and Ahaziah reveals how alliances and ambition erode devotion, yet God kept his covenant with David. His mercy restrains destruction and preserves a remnant. The Lord's purposes never collapse with human leadership; they rest on his character, not ours. Believers must therefore guard allegiance to God above convenience, refusing to let compromise disguise itself as wisdom. History's turbulence cannot undo heaven's promise. The lamp of David still burns because God's word endures forever—and that same word sustains the church amid moral decay today.

CONCLUSION

From floating iron to fleeing armies, from famine to restored families, these chapters reveal a God who sees and saves. Elisha's life proves that divine power is not limited to the battlefield or the palace. The same Lord who commands fiery chariots also redeems borrowed tools and grieving hearts. Faith's task is to look beyond fear and trust the unseen hand of God at work.

But even as God's mercy protected his people, corruption deepened in Israel and Judah. In the next lesson, judgment will arrive through Jehu—a man raised to end Ahab's legacy and purge idolatry from the land. The God who opens eyes in mercy would soon act in justice.

REFLECTION

1. What does the floating axe head teach about God's concern for ordinary needs?

2. How did Elisha's prayer open his servant's eyes to God's unseen protection?

3. Why did Elisha show mercy instead of vengeance to the captured Aramean soldiers?

4. How does the siege of Samaria reveal God's power to reverse human despair?

5. What do Elisha's tears for Hazael reveal about the prophet's understanding of God's justice?

6. How did Judah's alliance with Ahab's family threaten the promise to David's line?

DISCUSSION

1. How can we learn to see God's hand in everyday details and small concerns?

2. What helps believers develop faith that sees beyond fear?

3. When has God turned your discouragement into unexpected deliverance?

4. How can Christians share "good news" as boldly as the lepers of Samaria?

5. What lessons can we learn from Elisha's compassion toward his enemies?

6. How can the church remain faithful when culture and leadership around it decline?

5

JEHU & JUDGMENT
2 KINGS 9-10

Objective: To show that God's justice is sure, but only humble obedience brings lasting renewal.

INTRODUCTION

When a wildfire sweeps through a forest, it destroys everything in its path—but it also clears away years of decay and dead wood. After the flames die, new life can take root. Fire can both purge and scar.

Jehu's story burns across Israel's history like such a fire. Anointed by a prophet, he rode furiously from battlefield to palace, carrying out judgment on Ahab's wicked house. The blood of Naboth was avenged, Jezebel's arrogance ended, and Baal's temple fell. God's justice, long delayed, arrived in full. Yet beneath the smoke of victory lies another tragedy: Jehu's zeal for judgment never matured into obedience. He tore down one idol only to preserve another.

In these chapters, we see how divine wrath fulfills God's word—and how human pride can twist even holy work. The God of justice keeps every promise, but his servants must walk carefully, lest zeal become corruption. Jehu reminds believers that it is possible to fight for the right cause with the wrong heart.

This lesson explores the certainty of God's justice, the peril of partial obedience, and the truth that only repentance—not revolution—brings renewal. The Lord can use any tool to accomplish his will, but he delights in hearts that obey as well as act.

EXAMINATION

The anointing of Jehu (9:1–13)

The judgment promised against Ahab's house in Elijah's day came to pass through Jehu. Years earlier, God told Elijah to anoint Hazael king over Aram, Jehu king over Israel, and Elisha as his prophetic successor (1 Kgs. 19:15–17). Elijah anointed only Elisha, leaving the rest to his successor to complete. Now Elisha fulfilled the unfinished command.

The prophet sent one of the "sons of the prophets" to Ramoth-gilead with a flask of oil and urgent instructions. The young man found Jehu, a commander in Israel's army, took him aside, anointed him, and delivered a divine commission: "Thus says the Lord, the God of Israel, I anoint you king over the people of the Lord, over Israel. And you shall strike down the house of Ahab your master, so that I may avenge the blood of my servants the prophets" (vv. 6–7).

The anointing scene is swift and secretive—far different from Samuel's majestic ceremony with David. The prophet fled immediately, underscoring the danger of this act. Yet the oil poured in private would soon ignite a revolution.

Jehu stepped out, and his fellow officers, seeing the prophet's haste, asked what happened. When Jehu told them he had been anointed king, they wasted no time spreading cloaks beneath his feet and blowing trumpets, shouting, "Jehu is king!" (v. 13). The coup d'état began.

Jehu's story is one of divine purpose intertwined with human ambition. God uses flawed instruments to accomplish righteous judgment. Jehu's zeal was genuine, but his motives were mixed—part obedience, part opportunism. Peter Leithart notes that Jehu's anointing resembles the unleashing of divine wrath: "the oil that anoints also ignites." What follows will fulfill prophecy yet also expose the dangers of zeal without holiness.

The deaths of Joram and Jezebel (9:14–37)

Jehu wasted no time fulfilling his commission. Joram, Ahab's son, was recovering from battle wounds at Jezreel. With him was Ahaziah, king of Judah, whose alliance with Ahab's house sealed his fate. Jehu drove furiously toward the city, his chariot recognized from afar by its speed. When Joram rode out to meet him, he asked, "Is it peace, Jehu?" The answer was chilling: "What peace can there be, so long as the whorings and sorceries of your mother Jezebel are so many?" (v. 22).

Realizing the trap, Joram turned to flee, crying, "Treachery, O Ahaziah!" But Jehu drew his bow and shot him through the heart. His body was thrown onto Naboth's field, fulfilling Elijah's prophecy that Ahab's house would perish on that cursed ground (1 Kgs. 21:19). Ahaziah fled toward Megiddo but was struck down as well (v. 27).

Jehu then entered Jezreel, where Jezebel awaited. The queen, unbroken even in defeat, painted her eyes and adorned her head—perhaps to preserve dignity, perhaps to seduce or mock. From her window she taunted, "Is it peace, you Zimri, murderer of your master?" (v. 31). Her words recalled the earlier usurper Zimri, who reigned only seven days. Jezebel knew her history; she believed Jehu's rebellion would end the same way.

But her confidence was misplaced. Jehu called out, "Who is on my side? Who?" Two or three eunuchs appeared at the window. At his command, they threw her down. Her blood splattered the wall and the horses' hooves. Jehu trampled her corpse and went inside to eat and drink. Later, when he sent servants to bury her, they found only her skull, feet, and hands—the rest devoured by dogs, as Elijah foretold.

This scene epitomizes the grim fulfillment of divine justice: God's word never fails, even when its execution is horrific. Jezebel's end mirrors her crimes—blood for blood, arrogance consumed by humiliation. Jehu began his mission as God's avenger yet behaved with the same callous disregard for life that condemned Ahab's house. Divine judgment exposes sin but can also magnify it in the unrepentant.

Through Jehu, the Lord kept his promise, proving that evil rulers do not escape accountability. Yet the narrative also invites readers to tremble, not cheer. The Lord's vengeance is righteous, but the instrument's hands are not clean.

The purge of Ahab's house (10:1-17)

Jehu's revolution did not end with Jezebel. The northern kingdom still held dozens of Ahab's descendants in Samaria—seventy princes in all. Determined to fulfill his commission completely, Jehu wrote letters to the city's leaders, challenging them to select one of Ahab's sons, arm him, and fight for his dynasty. The officials, terrified, refused: "Behold, the two kings could not stand before him; how then can we stand?" (v. 4).

Jehu then issued a second letter ordering them to execute Ahab's sons themselves and deliver their heads in baskets to Jezreel. They obeyed. Seventy heads were piled at the city gate as proof that the purge was complete. Jehu stood before the grisly display and declared, "Know then that there shall fall to the earth nothing of the word of the Lord" (v. 10). In his mind, the slaughter vindicated prophecy and secured power.

Jehu next proceeded toward Samaria, killing all remaining relatives, courtiers, and priests of Ahab. On the way, he encountered the brothers of King Ahaziah of Judah—forty-two men traveling to visit the royal family—and ordered their deaths as well (vv. 12-14). His sword now cut through both kingdoms.

Jehu's zeal for judgment had become indiscriminate, driven as much by politics as prophecy. Though he fulfilled Elijah's commission, his motives were blurred. One writer calls him "God's scalpel turned sword"—useful for a moment but dangerous in hand. Jehu's reform cleanses the land with violence, but blood cannot cleanse the heart.

Despite his excess, Jehu also met a righteous ally. Jehonadab son of Rechab, a man known for piety and simplicity, joined him (vv. 15-17). Together they entered Samaria and completed the purge. Their alliance lent moral weight to Jehu's campaign, yet it couldn't sanctify its brutality. Jehonadab's presence highlighted what Jehu lacked—obedience born of humility rather than ambition.

The fall of Baal and the failure of Jehu (10:18-36)

Having removed Ahab's household, Jehu turned to Ahab's religion. He gathered the priests and worshipers of Baal, pretending to host a massive sacrifice in honor of the idol: "Ahab served Baal a little; Jehu will serve him much" (v. 18). His deceitful zeal drew every Baal devotee into the temple.

Once the doors were shut, Jehu's guards slaughtered them all. The temple was demolished, its pillars burned, and the site turned into a latrine (v. 27).

At first glance, Jehu seems the reformer Israel desperately needed. He eradicated Baal worship and fulfilled the word of the Lord given to Elijah. God even commended him partially: "Because you have done well in carrying out what is right in my eyes… your sons shall sit on the throne of Israel to the fourth generation" (v. 30). Yet the next verse exposes the tragedy: "But Jehu did not turn aside from the sins of Jeroboam, which he made Israel to sin" (v. 31).

Jehu's devotion ended where his self-interest began. He destroyed Baal but preserved the golden calves at Bethel and Dan—symbols of political control disguised as religion. His faith became selective obedience. Peter Leithart describes Jehu as a man who "executes the letter of God's word while missing its spirit." His chariot ran furiously but never faithfully. Jehu embodies a recurring biblical warning: zeal for judgment without zeal for holiness corrupts even the instruments of justice.

Under Jehu's rule, Israel's territory shrank as Hazael of Aram encroached on the north and east (vv. 32–33). The kingdom cleansed by violence began to crumble by violence. God's word was fulfilled, but Israel's heart remained unchanged. Jehu's story reminds readers that divine purposes can be accomplished through flawed instruments—but only holiness sustains blessing.

APPLICATION

1. God's justice is certain and complete

Jehu's story proves that the Lord's patience has limits and his promises never fail. Years after Elijah's prophecy, every word came true—Ahab's dynasty fell, Jezebel perished, and Baal's temple lay in ruins. God's justice may seem delayed, but it is never denied. Scripture teaches that divine judgment is not vengeance but faithfulness; the Lord keeps his word to defend the innocent and punish the guilty. In a world that trivializes sin, Christians must remember that God's justice is both inevitable and right. Yet his patience now calls us to repentance. Judgment delayed is mercy extended. The fall of Ahab's house reminds us to take sin seriously and to live with confidence that God's righteousness still rules history.

2. Zeal without obedience leads to corruption

Jehu's chariot thundered with zeal, but his heart lagged behind his mission. He executed judgment with precision yet preserved idolatry for convenience. Zeal alone cannot sustain holiness; passion must submit to obedience. Many believers begin with bold conviction but falter when obedience becomes costly. Jehu reminds us that partial faithfulness is disobedience dressed in religious clothes. God desires hearts, not headlines—steadfast devotion, not selective obedience. The Lord commended Jehu's actions but condemned his inconsistency. Christians today must beware of serving God's cause while neglecting God's commands. Righteous goals cannot justify unrighteous methods. True reform begins not with fury but with faithfulness, not with overthrowing others' idols but with surrendering our own.

3. God's imperfect instruments still answer to him

The Lord used Jehu's ambition to accomplish divine judgment, just as he once used Pharaoh's hardness and would use Cyrus's decree. God's sovereignty turns even flawed hearts into tools for his purpose. Yet usefulness is not approval. Jehu's success did not excuse his pride; his victories still faced divine evaluation. Christians should take comfort that God's plan is never thwarted by human weakness—but also take warning that participation in his work does not replace personal holiness. Preachers, leaders, and churches can achieve visible results and still displease the Lord if their motives are impure. Being God's instrument is not the same as being his disciple. Obedience, not outcome, is the measure of faithfulness.

4. Repentance, not revolution, brings renewal

Jehu cleansed Israel by force, yet the nation remained spiritually unhealed. Judgment removed idols, but repentance restores relationships. The same truth governs every generation: reform without renewal is temporary. Churches can build programs, purge traditions, or restructure leadership, but without humble repentance, revival will not come. God does not seek zeal that destroys but contrition that obeys. Jehu's failure warns against confusing outward change with inward conversion. The Lord desires mercy over sacrifice. Only hearts turned to him in faith will see lasting peace. Judgment exposes sin; repentance heals it.

CONCLUSION

Jehu's chariot thundered across Israel as the instrument of God's justice, but his legacy ended in compromise. Through him, God proved that sin never escapes judgment—but also that judgment alone cannot transform hearts. The Lord desires obedience rooted in humility, not zeal driven by ambition.

In the next lesson, the story turns from violence to preservation. Amid palace intrigue and bloodshed, a child-king named Joash will survive by God's providence, and a faithful priest will lead Judah back toward covenant renewal. The God who judges corruption in Israel will now protect the promise in Judah.

REFLECTION

1. Why was Jehu chosen to fulfill God's judgment against Ahab's house?
2. How did Jezebel's death demonstrate the certainty of God's word?
3. In what ways did Jehu's zeal both serve and distort God's purposes?
4. Why did God commend Jehu yet condemn his continued idolatry?
5. What does Jehu's alliance with Jehonadab reveal about true versus false obedience?
6. How does Jehu's story show that divine judgment alone cannot change human hearts?

DISCUSSION

1. How should believers balance confidence in God's justice with patience for his timing?
2. What are some modern examples of zeal without full obedience?
3. Why is it dangerous to confuse success in God's work with spiritual faithfulness?
4. How can churches pursue reform without losing compassion or humility?
5. What personal idols are easiest to justify in the name of good intentions?
6. Why is repentance more powerful than judgment in producing lasting renewal?

6

PRESERVATION & PROMISE
2 KINGS 11-12

Objective: To show that God preserves his promises through faithful people and calls believers to enduring obedience.

INTRODUCTION

In the early days of World War II, when London was bombed nightly, families sent their children away to the countryside for safety. Parents wept as trains carried their sons and daughters out of the city, trusting that protection in hidden places would preserve the future. History often turns on such acts of faith—quiet decisions that shelter tomorrow's hope.

Second Kings 11-12 tells a similar story. A ruthless queen named Athaliah tried to erase David's royal line, murdering her own grandchildren to seize power. Yet in one hidden room of the temple, a single child was spared. While evil reigned in the palace, God preserved the promise in secret. Years later, that child—Joash—would be crowned king, repair the temple, and renew the covenant of worship.

These chapters remind Christians that God's plans never die, even when threatened by chaos or corruption. His promises often survive through ordinary faithfulness—through hidden obedience, humble repair, and steadfast worship. The Lord who protected Joash still guards his church today.

This lesson explores how God preserved his covenant through courageous people, how renewal began in worship, and how faith must mature beyond borrowed conviction. The God who protects his promises in crisis still fulfills them in his time.

EXAMINATION

The queen who killed (11:1-3)

Athaliah's reign began with horror. When she saw that her son Ahaziah had been killed, she seized power by annihilating every possible heir to Judah's throne. Her slaughter was not merely political revenge—it was theological rebellion. By destroying David's line, Athaliah attempted to erase God's covenant itself. The promise of 2 Samuel 7, that a descendant of David would rule forever, hung by a thread. Judah's throne became the battleground between divine fidelity and human violence.

Yet God hides hope in the least likely place. Jehosheba, Ahaziah's sister and wife of Jehoiada the priest, risked her life to rescue the infant Joash. She concealed him in a bedchamber, then in the temple itself. For six years, the boy grew under priestly care, his cries echoing against the walls once defiled by Athaliah's Baal worship. The temple became a nursery, fortress, and symbol of covenant survival.

Athaliah's attempted genocide of David's heirs is the Old Testament's closest anticipation of Herod's massacre in Matthew 2—both moments where human pride struck at God's redemptive plan. When all seemed lost, God preserved his anointed under his own roof. The divine promise hid beneath the altar, waiting for its appointed hour.

Faithfulness here is quiet, domestic, and courageous. Jehosheba's decision stands beside Rahab's rescue and Moses' mother's defiance. Scripture reminds us that the kingdom's survival often depends on unseen obedience.

The priest who restored (11:4-21)

At last, when Joash turned seven, Jehoiada knew the time had come. The priest gathered captains, guards, and Levites in covenant secrecy. Their rebellion was meticulously ordered: one-third guarded the palace, one-third the gate, and one-third the temple. The precision underscores a vital truth—God's revolutions are not chaotic; they restore order under his word.

Jehoiada brought out the boy, placed a crown upon him, and gave him "the testimony"—a copy of the Law (v. 12). Kingship in Judah stood beneath Torah; the sword of authority bowed to the scroll of covenant. As trumpets sounded and the people cried, "Long live the king!", history turned from despair to deliverance.

Athaliah stormed into the temple, crying "Treason!", blind to her own. She was seized and executed outside the sanctuary, lest her blood profane it. The echo of Jezebel's fate resounded—another daughter of rebellion trampled under divine judgment.

Yet Jehoiada's triumph was not revenge but renewal. He made a threefold covenant between the Lord, the king, and the people: the nation would once again be the Lord's. Immediately the citizens demolished Baal's temple, shattered its altars, and slew its priest. The same city that once echoed with idolatrous chants now resounded with praise.

Jehoiada's leadership embodied godly reform: he restored worship before politics. The nation's stability flowed from covenant fidelity, not military victory. This episode teaches that God's promises are not kept through human might but through faithful intercession. While Athaliah sought security by bloodshed, Jehoiada secured peace through covenant. Renewal always begins with worship.

The king who repaired (12:1–16)

With the queen gone and peace restored, Judah experienced rare stability. Joash ascended the throne as a child saved by grace, shaped by Jehoiada's counsel. Scripture says, "Joash did what was right in the eyes of the Lord all his days because Jehoiada the priest instructed him" (v. 2). The phrasing is deliberate—his righteousness depended on relationship. As long as he listened, he prospered.

Joash's reign centered on rebuilding God's temple. Years of neglect under Athaliah had left the sanctuary scarred and looted. The king ordered that all silver from offerings be collected for repairs. Initially the priests failed to act, perhaps out of habit or fear, so Joash instituted a transparent system: a chest with a hole in its lid placed near the altar for public offerings. The money was counted by trusted officials and delivered directly to craftsmen—masons, carpenters, and metalworkers—who restored what had been desecrated.

The text emphasizes honesty: "They did not require an accounting from the men into whose hand they delivered the money to pay out to the workmen, for they dealt faithfully" (v. 15). In an era of corruption, integrity itself became a near-miracle.

This moment reveals the mundane side of faithfulness—record-keeping, construction, and stewardship. God's glory dwells not only in thunder but also in administration carried out with honesty. Theologically, Joash's repairs show how redemption moves from crisis to construction. After salvation comes service. The people who witnessed divine rescue had to rebuild what sin destroyed. Holiness requires maintenance as well as miracle. The temple's renewal thus prefigures the church's calling: to preserve purity and participate faithfully in God's ongoing work.

The faith that faltered (12:17–21)

Time, however, exposes the weakness of borrowed conviction. After Jehoiada's death, Joash lost his anchor. When Hazael of Aram invaded Judah, the king faced a choice: trust the God who preserved him or buy security with compromise. He chose the latter—emptying the temple of its sacred treasures, including the votive gifts of past kings, to pay off the enemy (v. 18).

The gesture secured temporary peace but signaled spiritual defeat. The temple that once symbolized covenant renewal now became a treasury for foreign power. Joash's fear undid his faith. Chronicles records that after Jehoiada died, Joash even turned to idolatry, ignoring prophetic warnings and ordering the stoning of Jehoiada's son Zechariah in the temple courtyard (2 Chr. 24:20–22). The boy whom the temple once saved now defiled it with blood.

Joash's story is a parable of dependence turned to defection. Guidance without conviction cannot endure. Jehoiada's mentorship gave Joash discipline but not devotion. Once the priest's voice fell silent, so did the king's conscience. His end is as tragic as it is instructive. Conspirators among his servants assassinated him at Beth-millo, the "House of Filling," a bitterly ironic name for an empty heart. He was buried in the city of David, but not among the royal tombs—a subtle verdict on a life that began in promise and ended in compromise.

Covenant preservation and human failure

Across these two chapters, a pattern emerges: divine faithfulness outlasts human failure. Athaliah's cruelty couldn't erase God's promise; Jehoiada's obedience restored it; Joash's corruption couldn't destroy it. The covenant thread wove through rebellion, reform, and relapse.

The contrast between Athaliah and Jehosheba, Jehoiada and Joash, mirrors the wider story of Israel and Judah—one generation killed the promise, another hid it, a third repaired it, and the fourth squandered it again. Yet through it all, God's purpose endured.

The narrative's rhythm of preservation and failure reminds us that God's grace is both protective and purifying. He guards his promise, but he also tests his people. The Lord's covenant is unconditional in endurance yet conditional in experience: the line of David survived, but each generation had to choose faithfulness to enjoy its blessings.

For modern readers, 2 Kings 11–12 teaches that divine preservation is not passive. God hides, raises, and restores his people through courageous obedience, communal reform, and persistent stewardship. But survival is not enough—faith must become personal conviction. The same God who protected infants in his temple calls adults to integrity in his service.

APPLICATION

1. God's promises survive when faith seems lost

Athaliah's massacre looked like the end of David's line, yet God's covenant survived in a hidden nursery. When human plans fail, divine promises still endure. God's faithfulness does not depend on visible strength or political control but on his unchanging word. Christians must remember that God's purposes are never in jeopardy, even when the world seems ruled by Athaliahs. The church may shrink, and truth may be silenced, but God always preserves a remnant. Our task is not to predict his methods but to trust his providence. The Lord who hid Joash in the temple still guards his promises in the hearts of faithful servants. His plan is never defeated; it is simply waiting for its appointed time to emerge.

2. Renewal begins in worship, not politics

Jehoiada's revolution was more spiritual than military. His first act after crowning Joash was not vengeance but covenant renewal. The priest led the people to rebuild the altar, restore the temple, and reaffirm loyalty to God. True reform begins with worship, not legislation. Modern Christians often seek revival through strategy or policy, but the heart of renewal is always returning to the Lord. Prayer, repentance, and worship accomplish what power cannot. The temple, not the palace, became the center of Judah's renewal. The same is true for the church today—our greatest influence comes from holiness, not dominance. Jehoiada reminds us that when God's people honor his covenant, peace follows and the land rejoices.

3. Stewardship is a form of faithfulness

Joash's temple repairs highlight that faith expresses itself in practical stewardship. The people's honest giving and the craftsmen's faithful work revealed hearts changed by gratitude. God delights in integrity as much as in sacrifice. The same Lord who accepted a widow's two coins honors labor done in faith. Christians today also repair God's house—not with stone and cedar, but through care for the church's mission and its people. Joash's reforms remind us that holiness includes honesty, diligence, and accountability. Every generation must rebuild what sin has neglected, giving time and resources to strengthen what sustains worship. When we labor faithfully for God's house, we demonstrate that his presence is our greatest treasure.

4. Borrowed faith cannot sustain obedience

Joash's faith thrived under Jehoiada's counsel but withered after the priest's death. His downfall warns that spiritual dependence on others cannot replace personal conviction. Guidance, mentorship, and community are vital, but faith must eventually stand on its own. When leaders fade, the heart must still trust God's word. Joash's compromise—trading temple treasures for political peace—exposes the danger of untested faith. Christians must move from inherited belief to intentional obedience, from borrowed conviction to personal devotion. Godly mentors point the way, but only individual faith endures trials. Like Joash, we are all sheltered by grace, yet called to grow into courage. The measure of maturity is not how well we follow another's example, but how faithfully we continue when that example is gone.

CONCLUSION

Through Athaliah's violence, Jehosheba's courage, Jehoiada's leadership, and Joash's wavering faith, one truth remained: God's promises endure. The Lord preserved David's line, restored his temple, and renewed his covenant despite human weakness. His faithfulness weaves through chaos, using ordinary people to protect extraordinary plans.

Yet Joash's fall reminds us that preservation must lead to perseverance. Borrowed faith cannot endure; conviction must be personal and steadfast. The same God who guards his promises calls his people to guard their hearts.

In the next lesson, we'll watch as God's mercy continues through generations of failing kings. Even when nations forget him, his covenant mercy remains the thread of hope holding history together.

REFLECTION

1. How did Athaliah's actions threaten God's covenant with David?
2. What qualities made Jehosheba's and Jehoiada's faith so courageous?
3. Why did Jehoiada prioritize covenant renewal before political reform?
4. How did Joash's temple repairs reveal genuine faith and integrity?
5. What caused Joash's obedience to collapse after Jehoiada's death?
6. How does this story demonstrate God's faithfulness through human failure?

DISCUSSION

1. Where have you seen God's promises endure despite human failure or opposition?
2. Why must spiritual renewal begin with worship instead of political or social reform?
3. How can Christians practice faithful stewardship in both ministry and daily life?
4. What habits help believers turn inherited faith into personal conviction?
5. How do mentors or spiritual leaders strengthen your obedience to God?
6. In what ways can the church today protect and nurture God's promises for the next generation?

7

MERCY IN THE MIDST
2 KINGS 13–15

Objective: To show that God's mercy endures through failure, calling his people to repentance and renewed faith.

INTRODUCTION

When a patient's heart weakens, a pacemaker keeps the rhythm steady even when the body falters. It doesn't cure the disease—it sustains life until something deeper changes. In Israel's later history, God's mercy functioned much the same way. The nation's spiritual heart was failing, yet divine compassion kept the pulse of promise beating.

In 2 Kings 13–15, both Israel and Judah staggered through cycles of sin and instability. Kings came and went—some weak, some violent, all flawed. Idolatry spread, borders shrank, and foreign threats loomed. Yet through every reign, God continued to show mercy. He delivered the oppressed, granted victory to unworthy leaders, and postponed judgment generation after generation. His compassion endures even when obedience disappears.

These chapters reveal that God's patience is not approval but purpose. He delays destruction so that repentance may still be possible. The Lord remains faithful, not because his people are consistent, but because his covenant is.

This lesson explores how mercy flows through decline, how faithlessness limits blessing, and how God's patience still calls his people back. In a world that often mistakes comfort for grace, Israel's story reminds believers that mercy is meant to heal, not to excuse.

EXAMINATION

Oppressed and delivered (13:1–9)

The reign of Jehoahaz, son of Jehu, opens with a familiar refrain: "He did what was evil in the sight of the Lord" (v. 2). Despite his father's zeal, Jehoahaz returned to the idolatry of Jeroboam I, maintaining the golden calves at Bethel and Dan. The pattern of partial reform and full relapse continued. As a result, God allowed Aram (Syria) to oppress Israel severely under King Hazael and his son Ben-hadad.

The text paints a bleak picture: Israel's once-mighty army was reduced to fifty horsemen, ten chariots, and ten thousand foot soldiers (v. 7). The people were cornered, humiliated, and helpless. Yet amid their misery, something remarkable happened. Jehoahaz "sought the favor of the Lord," and God "listened to him, for he saw the oppression of Israel" (v. 4). Divine compassion broke through where divine wrath had fallen.

This is one of Scripture's clearest portraits of undeserved mercy. Israel's repentance was shallow, yet God's compassion is deep. Their deliverance was not a reward for faithfulness but an act of grace to a suffering people. This episode mirrored the Exodus: God heard groaning under foreign bondage and acted to deliver, even when his people's hearts remained divided.

Still, the reprieve was incomplete. The nation continued its idolatry, "walking in the sins of Jeroboam." Mercy relieved their pain but did not reform their hearts. God's compassion is steadfast, but Israel's gratitude was short-lived. The Lord rescued, but the rescued returned to rebellion.

Arrows and bones (13:10–25)

The next scene shifts from Jehoahaz to his son Jehoash (Joash of Israel) and from political decline to prophetic legacy. Elisha, now aged and near death, received one final royal visitor. Jehoash wept over the dying prophet, crying, "My father, my father! The chariots of Israel and its horsemen!" (v. 14)—the same words Elisha once spoke at Elijah's departure. The phrase acknowledged that Israel's true defense lay not in armies but in God's prophetic word.

Elisha instructed Jehoash to take a bow and arrows, open a window eastward toward Aram, and shoot. The prophet declared, "The Lord's arrow of victory… over Syria!" (v. 17). Then he commanded the king to strike the ground with the remaining arrows. Jehoash did so three times and stopped. Elisha grew angry: "You should have struck five or six times… then you would have struck down Syria until you had made an end of it, but now you will strike down Syria only three times" (vv. 18–19).

This strange act exposed the limits of Jehoash's faith. His half-hearted obedience limited the scope of victory. God's promises require participation—he gives opportunity, but believers must respond fully. Jehoash's hesitation represented Israel's general spiritual lethargy: willing to obey in part but never in whole.

Elisha soon died, yet his ministry refused to end quietly. During a burial, raiders interrupted the funeral, and the mourners hastily tossed a dead man's body into Elisha's tomb. When the corpse touched the prophet's bones, the man revived and stood up (v. 21). The miracle demonstrated that even in death, God's word remains alive. His prophet's power transcended the grave.

The passage concludes with an account of ongoing warfare between Israel and Aram. Despite Israel's weakness, "the Lord was gracious to them and had compassion on them… because of his covenant with Abraham, Isaac, and Jacob" (v. 23). The covenant anchored mercy in promise, not performance. God's faithfulness outlived even his prophets and outlasts his people's failures.

This section illustrates resurrection hope in a dying kingdom. The living bones of Elisha anticipate the enduring life that flows from God's covenant. Where human faith falters, divine mercy breathes again.

Pride and defeat (14:1–22)

After the mercy shown to Israel in Jehoash's day, our attention turns south to Judah, where Amaziah, son of Joash, reigned. Like his father, he began well but finished poorly. The text says, "He did what was right in the eyes of the Lord, yet not like David his father" (v. 3). He obeyed the Law by executing his father's assassins but spared their children, honoring Deuteronomy 24:16. Yet his heart was divided—obedient in policy, prideful in spirit.

Amaziah's military success against Edom bred arrogance. He challenged Jehoash of Israel to battle, taunting, "Come, let us look one another in the face" (v. 8). The northern king replied with a parable about a thistle and a cedar: the weaker should not provoke the stronger. But Amaziah refused the warning. Judah was routed at Beth-shemesh, its walls torn down, its treasures looted, and the temple plundered (vv. 11–14).

Amaziah's pride marked a turning point—Judah's first serious humiliation since Jehoshaphat. The pattern of temporary obedience followed by self-confidence continued to plague both kingdoms. Amaziah was a moral echo of Saul—a man who obeyed selectively and confused victory with virtue.

Though Amaziah lived fifteen more years after Jehoash's death, his reign ended in conspiracy and exile. He fled to Lachish but was killed there, and his body was returned to Jerusalem for burial. The rise and fall of Amaziah illustrates a recurring biblical principle: pride always precedes downfall, even in those who begin with obedience. God resists the proud, whether in palaces or pulpits.

Prosperity and corruption (14:23–29)

Jeroboam II, Jehoash's son, succeeded him and reigned forty-one years—one of the longest tenures in Israel's history. Outwardly, it was a golden age. The kingdom expanded to its former borders, trade flourished, and prosperity returned. Yet the narrator immediately qualifies his success: "He did what was evil in the sight of the Lord. He did not depart from all the sins of Jeroboam the son of Nebat" (v. 24).

Despite Israel's idolatry, God acted in mercy: "The Lord saw that the affliction of Israel was very bitter… and had not said that he would blot out the name of Israel" (v. 26). So he saved them through Jeroboam's victories. Grace governed even national revival. Prosperity became another undeserved gift, not a reward for repentance.

Jeroboam's reign was mercy without renewal. The people enjoyed stability but remained spiritually hollow. Prophets like Amos and Hosea later condemned this same era for its complacent luxury and social injustice. Jeroboam II's kingdom was a glittering corpse—wealth without worship, growth without gratitude. Israel mistook divine patience for divine approval, a fatal confusion that has been repeated throughout history.

The chapter closes with God's quiet preservation: "The Lord saved them by the hand of Jeroboam" (v. 27). The same mercy that raised a dead man by Elisha's bones now raised a dying nation through an unfaithful king. God's compassion remained the only constant in Israel's revolving history of sin.

Kings and chaos (15:1–38)

Chapter 15 depicts the unraveling of both kingdoms. In Judah, Azariah (Uzziah) reigned long and well. He built cities, strengthened armies, and prospered. The Chronicler adds that "as long as he sought the Lord, God made him prosper" (2 Chr. 26:5). But pride infected success once again. Uzziah presumptuously entered the temple to burn incense—a priestly duty—and was struck with leprosy. He lived isolated, and his son Jotham governed in his stead. The king's skin disease became a living symbol of national contamination.

Meanwhile, the northern kingdom disintegrated into violence. Zechariah, Jeroboam II's son, ruled six months before assassination. Shallum reigned one month before Menahem murdered him. Menahem's cruelty was infamous: he ripped open pregnant women to suppress rebellion (v. 16). His reign survived only by paying heavy tribute to Assyria, marking the first appearance of the empire that would soon end Israel altogether.

After him, Pekahiah ruled briefly until Pekah killed him; then Pekah himself died by Hoshea's hand. In twenty years, Israel endured six kings, four coups, and no peace. The nation's moral collapse mirrored its political chaos. Power had replaced covenant, and survival had replaced faith. Yet even here, God allowed Israel time. The nation tottered but still stood. The Lord delayed final destruction, holding judgment in one hand and mercy in the other.

APPLICATION

1. God's mercy outlives our failures

Israel's history in these chapters shows that divine compassion does not depend on human worthiness. Jehoahaz prayed half-heartedly, yet God still heard. Jehoash struck too few arrows, yet God still granted victory. Again and again, the Lord's mercy outlasted Israel's rebellion. This is not leniency—it is covenant faithfulness. God remains who he is even when his people forget who they are. Christians today must guard against despair that assumes failure cancels grace. The cross proves that mercy endures where obedience collapses. Repentance, however weak, is still met with compassion. Our hope rests not in our consistency but in God's character. When sin leaves ruins behind, his mercy still rebuilds what pride destroyed.

2. Partial faith limits God's blessing

Jehoash's story of striking the arrows illustrates a sobering truth: half-hearted obedience receives half the blessing. God offered total victory, but the king's cautious faith achieved only partial success. The same pattern persists whenever believers approach God with minimal surrender—seeking safety, not transformation. The Lord's power flows through persistence, not hesitation. Prayer, faith, and service require wholehearted trust that God can do more than we imagine. Christians often miss spiritual victory because they stop short of full obedience. The lesson is not that God's grace depends on human effort, but that faith must respond fully to his word. Elisha's anger reminds us that God desires bold, expectant faith—faith that keeps striking the ground until his promise is complete.

3. Prosperity without holiness corrupts the soul

Jeroboam II's reign glittered with success but rotted with pride. Wealth and power masked spiritual decay. God's mercy gave prosperity, but Israel used it to indulge comfort instead of repentance. History—and the church—repeat this mistake when abundance breeds complacency. Material growth and social stability are not signs of divine approval; they are tests of stewardship. God's kindness should lead to humility, not indulgence. When comfort dulls our conscience, prosperity becomes judgment disguised as blessing. The people of Jeroboam's day mistook patience for permission. Christians must learn to view abundance as an opportunity to serve, not to boast. True gratitude measures success not by gain but by faithfulness. Holiness, not prosperity, defines blessing in the eyes of God.

4. God's patience has a purpose

The chaos of chapter 15 might seem like a slow-motion collapse, but divine delay is not divine neglect. God's patience is purposeful, giving space for repentance before judgment falls. Every coup, every act of cruelty, and every warning prophet was part of his mercy holding back final wrath. Yet patience is not endless; its goal is restoration. Israel's repeated instability proves that sin, when unrepented, will eventually self-destruct. For Christians, God's patience should inspire reverence, not presumption. When he withholds consequences, it is to call us back, not let us drift farther. The Lord's mercy invites change before his justice demands it. The lesson of these chapters is simple but urgent: do not mistake God's silence for approval. His patience waits for repentance, not rebellion.

CONCLUSION

Through fading kings and fractured kingdoms, one truth remains: God's mercy outlasts human failure. He hears even shallow prayers, revives the powerless, and delays judgment to give sinners time to return. Yet mercy unheeded becomes judgment delayed, not judgment denied. Israel's decline teaches that grace must lead to gratitude, or it will harden into presumption.

As the story continues, Judah will follow Israel's path toward captivity. In the next lesson, the final warning sounds—the northern kingdom will fall, and God's patience will yield to justice. But even in exile, mercy will not die, for the Lord still keeps his covenant.

REFLECTION

1. Why did God show mercy to Jehoahaz despite his continued idolatry?
2. What lesson does Jehoash's limited obedience with the arrows teach about faith?
3. How does Elisha's death scene illustrate the enduring power of God's word?
4. What led Amaziah from obedience to pride and eventual downfall?
5. How did Jeroboam II's prosperity reveal both God's compassion and Israel's corruption?
6. What does Israel's political chaos under Assyrian pressure reveal about God's patience?

DISCUSSION

1. How does God's mercy toward Israel encourage you when you feel spiritually inconsistent?
2. What are some modern examples of "partial faith" that limit God's blessings today?
3. How can churches remain faithful to God during times of material or social prosperity?
4. Why do people often confuse God's patience with his approval?
5. What helps you respond to God's mercy with repentance instead of complacency?
6. How can believers cultivate perseverance when God's deliverance seems delayed?

8

THE FALL OF THE NORTH

2 KINGS 16–17

Objective: To show that misplaced trust leads to ruin, but God's mercy endures beyond judgment.

INTRODUCTION

In 1912, the world watched in disbelief as the Titanic—a ship called "unsinkable"—vanished beneath the Atlantic. Confidence in human design gave way to catastrophe. Pride in technology blinded its builders to the danger of the sea. It was not the iceberg alone that doomed the ship, but misplaced trust.

The fall of Israel tells a similar story. For centuries the nation had drifted from covenant faith, trusting alliances, idols, and prosperity more than the God who brought them out of Egypt. When Assyria finally swept across the land, it was not merely political tragedy—it was divine consequence. The people who once bore God's name had exchanged worship for imitation and devotion for convenience.

In 2 Kings 16–17, Judah's king compromised with Assyria, and Israel's final king presided over the collapse. Yet even here, God's mercy glimmered through judgment. His patience has limits, but his purpose does not. Exile would purge, but not erase, his covenant promise.

This lesson explores how fear breeds compromise, how idolatry corrodes nations, and how mercy endures beyond destruction. The fall of the north was not the end of Israel's story—it was a new chapter in God's redemptive one.

EXAMINATION

Corruption in Judah (16:1-20)

Before Israel fell, Judah began to crumble from within. Ahaz, son of Jotham, ascended the throne at twenty years old and quickly abandoned his fathers' faith. Scripture states bluntly: "He did not do what was right in the eyes of the Lord his God" (v. 2). Instead of trusting God as David had, Ahaz imitated the nations, even sacrificing his own son in fire—an act once unthinkable in Judah.

When Rezin of Aram and Pekah of Israel allied against him, Ahaz faced a crisis of fear. Instead of turning to God, he turned to Assyria, sending gold and silver from the temple as a bribe for Tiglath-pileser III's help (vv. 7-8). His appeal succeeded militarily but destroyed Judah spiritually. By trusting empire over Yahweh, Ahaz traded covenant loyalty for political survival.

The king's apostasy deepened in Damascus, where he admired a pagan altar and ordered a replica built in Jerusalem (vv. 10-11). The bronze altar, once central to Israel's worship, was shoved aside. Ahaz rearranged temple furnishings and closed its entrances—literally reshaping sacred space to fit foreign taste. What began as fear ended as fashion; compromise became culture.

Ahaz's actions form the negative mirror of Hezekiah's coming reforms. He embodies Isaiah's warning that alliances with worldly power lead to ruin. Ahaz transformed the temple into a stage for Assyrian piety, showing how idolatry often enters not through rebellion but imitation. Judah's king sought relevance at the cost of reverence. By the chapter's end, Judah still stood politically, yet spiritually it resembled its northern neighbor. The house of David remained on the throne, but its faith lay dismantled beside a foreign altar. The seeds of exile were already sown in the temple courts.

The final king (17:1-6)

While Judah compromised, Israel collapsed. Hoshea, the last king of the northern kingdom, reigned nine years in Samaria. Compared to his predecessors, he "did evil, yet not as the kings of Israel who were before him" (v. 2). His moderation, however, couldn't save a nation long hardened in sin.

Initially, Hoshea served Assyria as a vassal, paying annual tribute to Shalmaneser V. But when he conspired with Egypt for freedom, the gamble failed. Assyria arrested him and besieged Samaria for three years. The city fell in 722 BC. The king was imprisoned; the people were deported; the land was emptied. The nation that once received God's covenant and prophets ceased to exist.

The narrator records the event with devastating simplicity: "So Israel was exiled from their own land to Assyria unto this day" (v. 23). Behind that sentence lies the fulfillment of centuries of warnings. From Jeroboam I's golden calves to Ahab's Baal, from Elijah's challenge to Elisha's tears, every prophetic word now converged in judgment.

The exile was not an accident of politics but the outworking of theology—God's righteous response to persistent idolatry. Assyria functioned as "Yahweh's rod," echoing Isaiah 10. The empire was powerful because God wielded it as an instrument of discipline.

The fall of Samaria proves that external success can mask internal decay. Israel had enjoyed military revival under Jeroboam II, but prosperity without repentance only delayed disaster. When divine patience reached its limit, the same Lord who once rescued Israel from Egypt now sent her back into bondage under foreign rule.

The fall explained (17:7–23)

After narrating Israel's collapse, the writer pauses for one of Scripture's most profound theological reflections. These verses explain why the northern kingdom fell—and why every generation must heed the same warning.

The cause was not Assyria's strength but Israel's sin: "And this occurred because the people of Israel had sinned against the Lord their God, who had brought them up out of the land of Egypt" (v. 7). The nation forgot its Redeemer. Idolatry replaced gratitude, and rebellion replaced covenant. They worshiped other gods, built high places, served Baal, and even sacrificed their children (vv. 9–17).

The text reads like an obituary of covenant failure. God sent prophets "to warn them," urging repentance, yet "they would not listen but were stubborn as their fathers had been" (vv. 13–14). The imagery evokes generations hardening their hearts like sun-baked clay. They rejected God's statutes, despised his commandments, and "went after false idols and became false" (v. 15). The tragedy is not merely that they worshiped what was empty but that they became what they worshiped.

Paul House calls this passage the theological heart of Kings, where history pauses to interpret itself. The narrator insists that exile was divine justice, not random misfortune. This reflection functions like a sermon: Israel's story became a warning to Judah and to every future reader. Grace rejected becomes judgment deserved.

The summary closes with a haunting refrain: "The Lord removed Israel out of his sight" (v. 18). The phrase does not imply God's blindness but his rejection of covenant intimacy. To be removed from his sight is to lose the privilege of his presence. Yet even here, the exile carried purpose. God's covenant judgment cleared the ground for a remnant to rediscover true worship. The surgeon's knife still belongs to the Great Physician.

A mixed people, a merciful God (17:24–41)

The Assyrians, following their imperial policy of population control, repopulated the emptied land with settlers from Babylon, Cuthah, and other conquered regions. These new inhabitants brought their gods with them, mixing local religion with imported superstition. When lions attacked the people, the king of Assyria interpreted it as divine anger: "The god of the land is displeased; send one of the priests to teach the law of the god of the land" (v. 27).

A priest returned from exile, teaching them "how they should fear the Lord," but the result was syncretism: "They feared the Lord but also served their own gods" (v. 33). The worship of Yahweh became one voice in a chorus of idols. A religion of convenience replaced covenant exclusivity.

This passage explains the later hostility between Jews and Samaritans. The mixed worship of this new population bred centuries of mistrust. Yet even this impure reverence showed that God's name could not be erased from the land.

The narrator repeats a refrain—"They do not fear the Lord as they should." True worship demands exclusivity; fear of the Lord cannot share space with compromise. Still, the very presence of God's instruction among foreigners testifies to lingering mercy. Though Israel's land was lost, their God remained active, teaching even those who replaced his people.

The chapter ends with both warning and hope: those who fear the Lord must live by his statutes; those who mix truth with idolatry will perish. The Lord may scatter his people, but he does not scatter his promise. His faithfulness outlasts even their faithlessness.

APPLICATION

1. Fear leads to compromise when faith falters

Ahaz feared men more than he trusted God. His panic before enemy armies opened the door to idolatry, imitation, and spiritual collapse. Fear often tempts believers to seek security in worldly power—politics, possessions, or popularity—rather than in God's promises. Yet compromise never produces peace; it only multiplies bondage. Faith calls us to courage even when the odds seem impossible. Judah's altar to Assyria warns that what we imitate, we soon worship. The answer to fear is trust rooted in covenant confidence: "If God is for us, who can be against us?" (Rom. 8:31). When fear demands we bow to culture's idols, faith must stand firm on God's word.

2. God's judgment is always just and redemptive

Israel's fall was not divine cruelty but divine consistency. God had warned, pleaded, and shown mercy for centuries before removing his people from the land. Judgment arrived only when mercy was exhausted by unrepentance. Scripture reminds us that God's justice is never impulsive; it is patient, purposeful, and righteous. His goal is always restoration, not revenge. Like a physician amputating to save life, God's judgment cuts to heal. Christians should tremble at sin's seriousness but also marvel at God's faithfulness. The exile proves that he keeps both warning and promise. When God disciplines his people today, it is not to destroy them but to draw them back to holiness. Judgment becomes grace when it drives us toward repentance.

3. True worship cannot be mixed

The settlers in Samaria feared the Lord but also served their own gods. That divided devotion remains a warning to every believer. The human heart is prone to mixture—blending faith with convenience, truth with culture, and obedience with self-interest. Yet the covenant demands exclusivity: "You shall have no other gods before me" (Exod. 20:3). The tragedy of the Samaritans was not ignorance but compromise. They wanted the blessings of Yahweh without surrender to his lordship. Christians today face similar temptations—to fear the Lord on Sunday but serve other masters through the week. Genuine faith cannot coexist with competing allegiances. Holiness requires separation from idols, whether of comfort, career, or control. God seeks hearts wholly devoted to him.

4. God's mercy endures even after collapse

When Israel vanished into exile, God's mercy did not vanish with them. Even in a land repopulated by foreigners, his name remained known, his law still taught, and his covenant still alive. The same God who judged also preserved. His mercy outlasts human ruin, turning despair into the soil of hope. Christians can take comfort that no failure, personal or national, lies beyond redemption. The cross proves that God still works beyond catastrophe. When life feels like exile—when faith falters and consequences fall—his mercy waits to rebuild what sin has torn down. Judgment may end a chapter, but grace always writes the next one. God's faithfulness outlives our failure, ensuring that his story never ends in ruin.

CONCLUSION

The fall of Israel stands as both warning and witness. It warns that compromise, idolatry, and misplaced trust will always end in exile—spiritually or nationally. Yet it also witnesses to God's unrelenting mercy. Even when his people are scattered, his covenant remains unbroken. Judgment clears the ground for grace to grow again.

As the story moves forward, hope shifts south to Judah, where another king will face the same Assyrian threat. In the next lesson, we'll see whether faith can stand where fear once fell. Hezekiah's courage will prove that trust in the Lord—not alliances, idols, or armies—is still the only path to deliverance.

REFLECTION

1. What does Ahaz's alliance with Assyria reveal about misplaced trust?
2. How does Hoshea's downfall show the danger of delayed repentance?
3. Why does the narrator emphasize Israel's covenant failure more than Assyria's power?
4. What key sins led to Israel's removal "from God's sight"?
5. How does the mixed worship in Samaria illustrate the peril of compromise?
6. In what ways does God's mercy continue even after Israel's exile?

DISCUSSION

1. What modern fears tempt Christians to compromise like Ahaz did?
2. How can God's discipline today reflect both his justice and his mercy?
3. In what ways do believers risk "fearing the Lord but serving other gods"?
4. How can churches guard against blending faith with cultural convenience?
5. Where have you seen God's mercy continue even after personal failure?
6. What does Israel's fall teach us about the urgency of repentance?

9

FAITH UNDER SIEGE
2 KINGS 18–19

Objective: To show that steadfast faith seeks God's glory and finds strength through prayer amid fear.

INTRODUCTION

During World War II, Winston Churchill addressed a frightened nation as bombs fell over London. He urged the people to stand firm, declaring, "We shall never surrender." Those words did not remove the danger—but they restored courage. In the darkest hours, faith in purpose gives strength when fear seems louder than reason.

Hezekiah faced a similar moment of crisis. The Assyrian empire had already crushed Israel, captured Judah's cities, and now surrounded Jerusalem. The world's most powerful army demanded surrender. Its spokesman mocked both king and God, claiming that faith was folly and resistance useless. Yet Hezekiah refused to panic. Instead, he turned to the only fortress the enemy could not breach—the presence of God.

In 2 Kings 18–19, we witness faith under siege: a king who reformed his nation, prayed under threat, and trusted in a deliverance only God can provide. The Lord's answer—an overnight victory—reveals that faith's defense is never in strength but in surrender.

This lesson explores what courage looks like when fear shouts the loudest. Hezekiah's story reminds Christians that when faith bends its knees, the world's mightiest threats must bow before God's power.

EXAMINATION

Reform and resolve (18:1–12)

Hezekiah's reign began as a bright dawn after years of twilight. Unlike his father Ahaz, who desecrated the temple and imported Assyrian worship, Hezekiah recentered Judah's life on the Lord. Scripture declares, "He trusted in the Lord … so that after him there was none like him among all the kings of Judah" (v. 5). His first acts were radical reforms: he removed high places, broke the pillars, cut down the Asherah, and even destroyed the bronze serpent that Moses had made because it had become an idol (v. 4).

This was reformation without hesitation. Hezekiah understood that half-obedience was still disobedience. His cleansing of the land reversed Ahaz's compromise, proving that true leadership begins with loyalty to God, not alliance with power. Hezekiah's destruction of the bronze serpent reveals a key truth—even sacred things must die when they become substitutes for God.

Yet reform soon met resistance. Assyria, the empire Ahaz once courted, now threatened Judah. In 701 BC, Sennacherib invaded, seizing fortified cities and demanding tribute. Hezekiah initially paid by stripping silver and gold from the temple (vv. 14–16), a moment of weakness that shows even the faithful can falter under pressure. Still, the narrative emphasizes his general trust: "The Lord was with him; wherever he went he prospered" (v. 7).

Hezekiah's reign presents a living contrast to Israel's fall in 17: both nations faced Assyria—one collapsed in fear, the other stood in faith. Reform rooted in trust became the foundation for endurance under siege.

Taunts and terror (18:13–37)

The Assyrian army soon surrounded Jerusalem. Sennacherib sent his field commander, the Rabshakeh, to deliver psychological warfare. Standing by the conduit of the upper pool—the very spot where Isaiah once met Ahaz (Isa. 7:3)—the scene became a deliberate echo of history. Where Ahaz refused to trust God, Hezekiah now decides differently.

The Rabshakeh's speech is a masterpiece of intimidation. He mocked Hezekiah's faith: "Do you think mere words are strategy and power for war?" (v. 20). He ridiculed Egypt's alliance as a broken reed and then derided trust in the Lord: "Has any god of the nations delivered his land from the hand of the king of Assyria?" (v. 33). His rhetoric was cunning—half-truths wrapped in logic, aimed at turning confidence into despair.

The speech oozes with serpent theology—words that sound reasonable but poison the heart. The Rabshakeh redefined faith as folly and obedience as weakness. He spoke loudly "in the language of Judah" so the people on the wall would hear, a deliberate attempt to spread panic.

Hezekiah's officials—Eliakim, Shebna, and Joah—begged him to speak in Aramaic, not Hebrew, but he refused, shouting louder. He promised the people security, vineyards, and peace if they surrendered. His offer mirrored the serpent's promise in Eden: life apart from God.

Through it all, the people remained silent. Hezekiah had commanded, "Do not answer him" (v. 36). Their silence became an act of faith—a refusal to debate unbelief on its own terms. Their restraint marked a turning point: Judah finally learned what Israel never did—to let God, not fear, have the last word.

The chapter ends with tension. Hezekiah's officers tore their clothes, returning to the king with the Rabshakeh's words—words that would soon drive the king to prayer instead of panic.

Prayer and promise (19:1–19)

When fear filled the city, Hezekiah's first response was not strategy but surrender. He tore his clothes, covered himself in sackcloth, and entered the temple of the Lord. This is the same temple his father had defiled for political gain; now it became a house of prayer and refuge.

He sent his officials to Isaiah, confessing, "This day is a day of distress, of rebuke, and of disgrace; children have come to the point of birth, and there is no strength to bring them forth" (v. 3). The image of labor without strength captures the nation's helplessness—Judah was on the verge of collapse, unable to deliver itself.

Isaiah's reply was brief but decisive: "Do not be afraid because of the words that you have heard… I will put a spirit in him, so that he shall hear a rumor and return to his own land" (vv. 6–7). Faith is not strengthened by ignoring fear but by hearing God's word above it.

Soon, Sennacherib sent another message—a blasphemous letter claiming that no god has ever saved a nation from Assyria's power. Hezekiah went again to the temple, spread the letter before the Lord, and prayed one of the Bible's most beautiful petitions: "O Lord, the God of Israel, enthroned above the cherubim, you are the God, you alone, of all the kingdoms of the earth; you have made heaven and earth… Now, O Lord our God, save us, please, from his hand, that all the kingdoms of the earth may know that you, O Lord, are God alone" (vv. 15–19).

This prayer represents the center of Hezekiah's faith and the heart of the theology of Kings. It shifted the focus from national survival to divine glory. Hezekiah's concern was not for his reputation but for God's. His posture—spreading the letter before God—embodies faith made visible: he literally laid his fear at the feet of the Almighty. When threats grow loud, true faith grows quiet and kneels.

Deliverance and defeat (19:20–37)

Isaiah delivered the Lord's answer in a powerful oracle. God first addressed Sennacherib's arrogance directly: "Whom have you mocked and reviled? Against whom have you raised your voice? Against the Holy One of Israel!" (v. 22). The king who boasted of his conquests learned that every step of his armies was decreed by the Lord he ridiculed: "Have you not heard that I determined it long ago?" (v. 25).

The tone shifts from accusation to assurance. God promised that Sennacherib would not enter Jerusalem, shoot an arrow there, or even build a siege ramp. "By the way that he came he shall return… For I will defend this city to save it, for my own sake and for the sake of my servant David" (vv. 32–34).

That night, the angel of the Lord struck down 185,000 soldiers in the Assyrian camp. The invincible army was undone without a single sword from Judah. When morning came, the besiegers were corpses. Sennacherib withdrew to Nineveh, and years later his own sons assassinated him while he was worshiping his idol. The one who mocked God died in the shadow of false worship.

This victory vindicated faith as realism—not wishful thinking, but confidence in the sovereign Lord who rules empires and armies alike. The scene closes quietly, yet triumphantly: Jerusalem stood, untouched, surrounded not by enemies but by evidence of God's power. The prayer of one faithful king silenced the mightiest empire on earth.

APPLICATION

1. Genuine faith requires courageous reform

Hezekiah's first act as king was not building armies or alliances—it was restoring worship. He tore down idols, destroyed sacred objects, and purified the temple. His courage reminds believers that faith begins with cleansing, not compromise. Reform often requires confronting traditions or comforts that have quietly replaced devotion. Like Hezekiah, we must dismantle anything that competes for God's throne, even if it once seemed good. The life of faith begins with repentance, and spiritual renewal often means making hard choices. When Christians return to wholehearted worship, God restores purpose and power. Reform may invite opposition, but it also prepares the way for victory.

2. Faith listens to God's word when fear speaks loudest

The Rabshakeh's taunts were crafted to break confidence—mocking faith, reason, and hope. Hezekiah's people resisted not by argument but by silence, waiting for God's answer. True faith doesn't match fear's volume; it listens for God's voice instead. When threats surround us—financial, relational, cultural—faith must tune its ear to Scripture, not the noise of despair. The world's logic says, "You're alone and powerless." God's truth replies, "I am with you always." Hezekiah's restraint teaches that faith refuses to debate lies on their terms. Believers don't need louder voices but deeper trust. When fear speaks, the faithful turn their attention to the Word that cannot fail.

3. Prayer is the refuge of the faithful

When the siege tightened, Hezekiah didn't run to Egypt or the armory—he went to the temple. His prayer redefined crisis as opportunity for worship. He spread Sennacherib's letter before the Lord, proving that faith takes worries to the only One who can do something about them. Prayer turns panic into peace because it moves the burden from our hands to God's. Like Hezekiah, believers can bring every accusation, every fear, and every impossibility into the Lord's presence. Prayer is not escape from battle—it is the battlefield where victory begins. When we kneel before God, no enemy can stand against us. Faith finds its strength not in defiance but in dependence.

4. God delivers for his glory, not our comfort

The Lord saved Jerusalem not because Hezekiah deserved it, but because God's name deserved honor. His deliverance preserved the covenant and displayed his power to the nations. Christians must remember that God's rescue always serves his redemptive purpose, not merely our relief. We pray for help, but his goal is holiness. When he answers, it's to reveal his character through our weakness. Hezekiah's victory shows that faith's reward is not comfort but communion—the experience of God's faithfulness in the midst of fear. Every trial becomes a stage for his glory. The same God who defended Jerusalem still defends his people today, proving that salvation belongs to him alone.

CONCLUSION

Hezekiah's story proves that faith under siege does not crumble—it kneels. When the Rabshakeh mocked, when fear surrounded, and when strength failed, the king spread his fears before the Lord. God's answer was not merely deliverance but revelation: the Holy One of Israel reigns above every empire. True victory belongs to those who trust God's word more than the world's threats. Prayer remains the fortress of faith and the pathway to peace.

In the next lesson, we'll see Hezekiah's faith tested again—this time not by armies, but by pride and mortality. The king who trusted God in crisis must now trust him in success.

REFLECTION

1. What set Hezekiah's reforms apart from those of previous kings?
2. How did the Rabshakeh's words challenge both reason and faith?
3. Why did Hezekiah command the people to remain silent before their enemy?
4. What does Hezekiah's prayer reveal about his view of God's character?
5. How does God's response through Isaiah emphasize divine sovereignty over nations?
6. What parallels exist between Hezekiah's deliverance and Israel's Exodus story?

DISCUSSION

1. What idols or habits might God be calling you to tear down in your life?
2. How can believers train their hearts to hear God's voice above fear's noise?
3. What does Hezekiah's example teach about responding to threats or criticism?
4. Why is prayer more powerful than strategy when faith feels surrounded?
5. How can we make sure our prayers seek God's glory, not just our comfort?
6. What does Hezekiah's story teach about trusting God when deliverance seems impossible?

10

FAITH & FRAILTY

2 KINGS 20-21

Objective: To show that God's mercy restores the humble, but pride and neglect destroy faith's legacy.

INTRODUCTION

In the Rocky Mountains, climbers often speak of "summit blindness." After hours of strain, the moment they glimpse the peak, they grow careless. The same focus that carried them upward fades when the goal seems near. More accidents happen on descents than ascents—not because the path changed, but because the climber did.

Hezekiah's life reflects that same danger. After years of faithful reform and miraculous deliverance, he faced one last test—not a battlefield, but his own heart. When illness struck, he prayed with tears and received fifteen more years of life. Yet the mercy that restored him soon became the stage for pride. And after his reign, his son Manasseh undid everything his father had built.

Second Kings 20–21 reveals the frailty of even the strongest faith when gratitude fades into self-confidence. God's mercy is generous, but it is never a license for pride. The same Lord who extends life also holds every generation accountable for how it's lived.

This lesson explores the mercy that restores, the pride that ruins, and the faith each generation must claim for itself. The God who healed Hezekiah and judged Manasseh still calls his people to humility, holiness, and endurance.

EXAMINATION

Healing and humility (20:1–11)

Hezekiah's story, which began with triumph over Assyria, now turns inward. The king who once faced armies now faced mortality. The text opens bluntly: "In those days Hezekiah became sick and was at the point of death" (v. 1). The prophet Isaiah delivered a devastating message: "Set your house in order, for you shall die; you shall not recover."

Hezekiah's reaction was immediate and raw. He turned his face to the wall and prayed, weeping bitterly: "Remember, O Lord, how I have walked before you in faithfulness and with a whole heart" (v. 3). God answered before Isaiah left the courtyard: the prophet had to return with a new word—fifteen more years of life and deliverance from Assyria's threat.

This passage displays both God's mercy and Hezekiah's humanity. Faith does not erase fear, but it transforms it into prayer. Hezekiah's tears reveal dependence, not doubt. His life, once extended by divine grace, became a living parable of God's compassion.

As a sign, God caused the shadow in the palace to move backward ten steps. The miracle reversed time's natural flow, symbolizing divine power to undo what seems irreversible. Just as the "clock" turned back, God reversed the sentence of death. The same Lord who halted the sun for Joshua now bent time itself to answer prayer.

Yet this healing carried a subtle warning. The chapter's structure mirrors Israel's own story—rescued from peril, blessed by mercy, but soon tempted by pride. The gift of added years became a test of the heart.

Pride and prophecy (20:12–21)

Not long after his recovery, Hezekiah faced a different test—prosperity. Envoys arrived from Babylon, sent by King Merodach-baladan, ostensibly to congratulate him on his healing. But beneath their courtesy lay curiosity. Babylon, still a rising power, sought an alliance and intelligence against Assyria.

Flattered by their attention, Hezekiah welcomed them eagerly and showed them everything: "all his treasure house, the silver, the gold, the spices, the precious oil, his armory, all that was found in his storehouses" (v. 13). The king who once laid his fears before God now laid his treasures before men.

Isaiah's response pierced the illusion of success: "Hear the word of the Lord... Behold, the days are coming when all that is in your house... shall be carried to Babylon" (vv. 16–17). The prophet's words turned Hezekiah's display into prophecy—the very wealth he flaunted would one day become spoils of exile.

This story parallels Ahaz's earlier failure in chapter 16. Both kings forgot that God's favor, not political skill, sustained the throne of David. Hezekiah's pride was subtle, not scandalous. It arose not from rebellion but relief. Having survived one crisis, he let success dull dependence.

Hezekiah's final response is complex. He accepted Isaiah's word humbly but selfishly: "The word of the Lord that you have spoken is good... for there will be peace and security in my days" (v. 19). He submitted to judgment but did not lament its impact on future generations.

The king who once prayed for life now resigned himself to survival. His final years remind readers that faith must be renewed as surely as health. Past victories cannot sustain present humility.

Reversal and ruin (21:1–18)

The story shifts from Hezekiah's devotion to his son Manasseh's depravity—a jarring transition that highlights how quickly faith can unravel across generations. Manasseh began his reign at twelve years old and ruled for fifty-five years, the longest in Judah's history. Yet his longevity only multiplied his evil.

Scripture spares no detail: "He rebuilt the high places that Hezekiah his father had destroyed, erected altars for Baal, made an Asherah, and worshiped all the host of heaven" (vv. 3–5). He even built pagan altars inside the temple, the very place where God declared, "In Jerusalem I will put my name" (v. 4). What Hezekiah cleansed, Manasseh contaminated. The king led Judah to do "more evil than the nations" the Lord had expelled before them (v. 9).

Manasseh's reign represents the theological undoing of everything Hezekiah accomplished. The son reversed every reform, turning covenant faith into national apostasy. He even practiced sorcery, consulted mediums, and sacrificed his own son—a grotesque echo of Ahaz. The royal palace became the epicenter of rebellion.

God's response was uncompromising: "I am bringing upon Jerusalem and Judah such disaster that the ears of everyone who hears of it will tingle" (v. 12). The Lord would "wipe Jerusalem as one wipes a dish, wiping it and turning it upside down." The image captures total judgment—complete reversal, complete cleansing.

Manasseh's sin made Judah the new Canaan: the chosen people became like the nations they replaced. Covenant privilege without covenant obedience invites covenant curse. The exile, which seemed distant in Hezekiah's day, now became inevitable. Manasseh was buried in his garden rather than among the kings of Judah. The man who filled Jerusalem with idols found no resting place near God's temple.

A legacy of decline (21:19–26)

Manasseh's son Amon continued the pattern of rebellion. His reign lasted only two years but confirmed the nation's downward spiral. The text mirrors his father's description almost word for word: "He walked in all the way in which his father walked and served the idols that his father served" (v. 21).

Amon's end was swift and symbolic. His servants conspired and assassinated him in his house, but the people killed the conspirators and placed his son Josiah on the throne (v. 24). The cycle of sin and violence consumed even the palace, yet beneath the chaos, God's providence still moved. Out of this wreckage would rise a reformer greater than Hezekiah—Josiah, the final bright flame before Judah's exile.

Amon's short reign proves a sobering truth: evil can destroy faster than righteousness can rebuild. Generations may labor for renewal, but rebellion can erase their work overnight. Judah's story has reached a moral freefall: the kingdom no longer drifts but nosedives. Each reign accelerates judgment, and the tone of the narrative darkens toward inevitable exile.

Still, hope lingers between the lines. God preserved a royal line through which his promise to David would endure. The covenant lamp flickered but would not go out. The same God who extended Hezekiah's life and judged Manasseh's sin remained faithful to his redemptive plan.

APPLICATION

1. God's mercy meets honest prayer

When Hezekiah faced death, he turned his face to the wall and wept before God. His prayer was not polished but personal—a cry of desperation anchored in faith. God's swift answer reminds believers that prayer still moves the heart of heaven. Yet Hezekiah's healing also teaches that mercy is a gift, not a guarantee. Each added day is grace, meant for gratitude and renewed service. Christians should remember that divine compassion responds not to merit but to dependence. The God who extended Hezekiah's life still listens to prayers whispered in weakness. When faith kneels in honesty, God delights to show mercy that defies expectation.

2. Pride is the subtle enemy of the faithful

Hezekiah's greatest test came not in crisis but in comfort. Babylon's envoys offered flattery, and the king—once humble in sickness—became boastful in health. Pride often enters quietly, after victory, when self-sufficiency replaces surrender. Like Hezekiah, believers must guard their hearts in success as carefully as in suffering. Every accomplishment is an opportunity for worship or arrogance. The moment we display God's gifts as our own, we begin to lose them. The faithful learn that gratitude keeps success holy. The same God who grants blessing demands that it be held with humility. Pride is healed only by remembering who truly owns the treasure.

3. One generation's faith cannot substitute for another's

Manasseh's reign proves that faith is not inherited. A godly father cannot believe on behalf of his son. Spiritual legacy must be chosen, not assumed. Hezekiah's reforms created opportunity, but Manasseh's choices revealed a rebellious heart. Every generation must rediscover God's truth for itself. Churches and families must therefore train faith, not tradition—hearts, not habits. It is not enough to rebuild temples if children still love idols. Parents can model conviction and teach Scripture, but only personal surrender keeps faith alive. The contrast between Hezekiah and Manasseh warns believers that neglecting discipleship invites decline. What one generation prays for, the next must practice—or it will perish.

4. God's judgment is severe but never faithless

Manasseh filled Jerusalem with blood, yet God's justice still served his covenant purpose. The Lord declared he would wipe the city clean—not out of cruelty but to purge corruption. Judgment was not abandonment but purification. Even in wrath, God remains righteous and true. His discipline always aims to restore holiness, never to destroy hope. Christians should remember that divine patience has limits, but divine promise never fails. When sin multiplies, judgment becomes mercy in disguise—a reset for redemption. The fall of Judah would pave the way for a remnant and, ultimately, for the Messiah. God's faithfulness outlasts even his people's rebellion. He is severe in order to save.

CONCLUSION

Hezekiah's story ends where all faith must begin—with mercy—and Manasseh's reign ends where pride always leads—with ruin. One king prayed and received life; the other rebelled and brought death to his nation. Yet even in judgment, God's covenant promise endured. His mercy does not depend on perfect leaders but on his unchanging faithfulness.

These chapters remind Christians that every generation must renew its devotion. Yesterday's obedience cannot sustain today's heart. The God who healed Hezekiah and judged Manasseh still calls his people to humility and repentance.

In the next lesson, a young king named Josiah will rediscover God's law and ignite one final revival before exile. Grace, though often forgotten, will again find a willing heart.

REFLECTION

1. What does Hezekiah's prayer teach about God's response to honest dependence?
2. Why did God give Hezekiah a miraculous sign through the shadow's reversal?
3. How did pride change Hezekiah's attitude after his recovery?
4. In what ways did Manasseh undo his father's reforms?
5. What does God's judgment against Manasseh reveal about covenant accountability?
6. How does Judah's decline illustrate the danger of forgetting generational faith?

DISCUSSION

1. How can believers learn to pray with the same honesty and humility as Hezekiah?
2. What signs of pride can quietly appear after seasons of success or answered prayer?
3. How can families and churches help the next generation develop personal, lasting faith?
4. Why is God's judgment both necessary and redemptive in Scripture's story?
5. What safeguards can keep gratitude from turning into self-reliance?
6. How does remembering God's mercy help us endure his discipline?

11

THE BOOK & THE KING

2 KINGS 22:1–23:30

Objective: To show that revival begins when God's word is rediscovered, believed, and obeyed from the heart.

INTRODUCTION

In 1947, a Bedouin shepherd tossed a stone into a cave near the Dead Sea and heard pottery shatter. Inside, he found clay jars containing ancient manuscripts that became known as the Dead Sea Scrolls. What had been hidden for centuries suddenly spoke again, reigniting understanding of Scripture's history. Sometimes God restores truth not by revealing something new, but by returning what was lost.

Josiah's story begins with a similar discovery. During temple repairs, a priest found a forgotten scroll—the Book of the Law. When it was read to the young king, its words pierced him to the heart. He tore his robes in grief, realizing how far Judah has strayed from covenant faithfulness. That rediscovered book transformed a nation, reminding God's people that revival begins when the word of the Lord reclaims its rightful place.

In 2 Kings 22–23, Josiah's encounter with Scripture sparked repentance, reform, and renewal. He became the model of wholehearted devotion—leading the people to destroy idols, restore worship, and renew covenant loyalty. Yet his death also revealed the limits of human reform: law can guide, but only grace can save.

This lesson explores how rediscovering God's word revives faith and how obedience keeps revival alive.

EXAMINATION

Rediscovery and repentance (22:1–20)

Josiah's story begins like a sunrise breaking over long darkness. After the evil of Manasseh and Amon, the narrator's opening words signal hope: "He did what was right in the eyes of the Lord… and did not turn aside to the right or to the left" (22:2). The phrase echoes Deuteronomy 5:32, identifying Josiah as the ideal covenant king—the one who finally lives by the book before he even finds it.

At eighteen years old, Josiah ordered repairs on the neglected temple. Faithfulness expressed itself not in speeches but in stewardship. As workers gathered funds and restored the sanctuary, the high priest Hilkiah made a discovery that would reshape Judah's history: "I have found the Book of the Law in the house of the Lord" (v. 8).

The text does not specify which book, but context points to Deuteronomy—the covenant manual of obedience and blessing. When Shaphan the scribe read it to the king, Josiah's response was immediate: he tore his clothes in grief (v. 11). The word confronted him with sin accumulated over centuries. His humility mirrored Hezekiah's prayer but deepened it—Hezekiah sought life; Josiah sought forgiveness.

This was the rediscovery of divine expectation. God's people cannot serve him rightly until they rediscover what he actually requires. Josiah's repentance shows how the word functions: it kills before it heals. The law reveals guilt before grace restores.

Unsure how to respond, Josiah sent a delegation to the prophetess Huldah, seeking confirmation of God's will. Her message came in two parts—judgment and mercy. Judgment: Judah's idolatry had gone too far; the covenant curses would fall. Mercy: Josiah himself would die in peace because his heart was tender, and he humbled himself before the Lord (vv. 16–20).

Huldah's oracle demonstrates that true repentance does not cancel consequences but transforms how one faces them. God's wrath would come, yet the king's humility delayed it. Josiah's generation received a reprieve, not a pardon—proof that repentance may not erase history but can still redeem the present.

For Judah, the rediscovery of the word began a short-lived revival. For readers, it reveals a timeless pattern: reformation always begins when God's word is rediscovered, read, and obeyed.

Renewal and reading (23:1–3)

Josiah's repentance became public renewal. He gathered elders, priests, prophets, and people—"both small and great"—and personally read the Book of the Covenant aloud (23:2). The king who once heard now proclaimed. The word that broke him now bound the nation.

This moment is the spiritual climax of Kings. The scene deliberately mirrors Sinai: a people gathered, a covenant read, vows renewed. Standing by the pillar (a symbol of divine presence and royal accountability), Josiah lead by example: "He made a covenant before the Lord, to walk after the Lord and to keep his commandments... with all his heart and all his soul" (v. 3). The language echoes Deuteronomy 6:5, the Shema—the command to love God fully.

Josiah embodied ideal kingship: he did not impose reform by decree; he modeled it through surrender. His reading of the law reestablished the temple as the nation's spiritual center and the word as its moral constitution. Worship and obedience were no longer separated; they were fused in covenant renewal.

The people's response, "All the people joined in the covenant," shows the power of leadership rooted in conviction. One heart ignited by Scripture can awaken a nation. Yet the passage's tension remains: would this renewal endure? For now, the Book had found its king, and the king had found his God.

Reform and purge (23:4–20)

Covenant renewal quickly became covenant action. Josiah's repentance was not sentimental—it was surgical. He moved from hearing the word to purging the land. His reforms began at the temple, then rippled outward through Jerusalem and across the nation.

He commanded Hilkiah and the priests to remove from the temple all vessels made for Baal, Asherah, and the "host of heaven." These were burned outside Jerusalem, their ashes carried to Bethel—the very heart of northern apostasy (v. 4). The king tore down the idolatrous shrines his ancestors had tolerated, defiled the altars that kings had built, and even destroyed the "houses of male cult prostitutes" beside the temple (vv. 5-7).

Josiah's purge fulfilled Deuteronomy's command to "destroy" false worship (Deut 12:2-4). His zeal embodied covenant obedience—an all-encompassing rejection of anything that competes with God. Josiah reversed Solomon's downfall: the idols once built by Solomon's compromise were now shattered by Josiah's devotion.

The reforms extended into Samaria, the territory of the fallen northern kingdom. There, Josiah broke down the altar at Bethel, the very shrine established by Jeroboam I. He burned human bones on the altar, fulfilling the prophecy given three centuries earlier in 1 Kings 13:2—the one naming Josiah before his birth. The historian's inclusion of this scene shows that God's word governs history down to the name of the reformer.

Josiah was a new Joshua, conquering idolatry instead of Canaan. Yet his campaign, though thorough, couldn't cleanse hearts. External reform cannot guarantee internal renewal. The nation's obedience still depended on individuals embracing covenant truth personally. Josiah purified worship, but he couldn't produce repentance in the generations to come. Still, for a brief and brilliant moment, the word of God ruled again in Judah.

Passover and passing (23:21-30)

After cleansing the land, Josiah restored the feast that celebrated deliverance. He commanded, "Keep the Passover to the Lord your God, as it is written in this Book of the Covenant" (v. 21). For the first time since the days of the judges, Israel observed Passover in its full biblical form. Worship returned to the word; celebration became remembrance of redemption.

This Passover was the theological heart of Josiah's reform. It reaffirmed that salvation is God's act and worship is the fitting response. The king's devotion united people, priests, and prophets under one law.

The narrator crowns Josiah with the highest praise given to any ruler in 1-2 Kings: "Before him there was no king like him, who turned to the Lord with all his heart and with all his soul and with all his might" (v. 25). The language directly mirrors Deuteronomy 6:5, identifying Josiah as the ultimate Deuteronomic king (arguably greater than David). His life embodied the ideal that the law demanded and most kings ignored.

Yet the story ends in tragedy. Despite his faith, the Lord's wrath still "did not turn from the burning of his great anger" (v. 26). The cumulative guilt of Manasseh's sins couldn't be undone. Josiah died in battle at Megiddo, struck down by Pharaoh Neco (v. 29). His death marked the end of Judah's independence and the beginning of Babylon's shadow.

APPLICATION

1. Revival begins with God's word

Josiah's renewal started not with emotion or policy but with the rediscovery of scripture. The word of God, long forgotten, proved powerful enough to convict a king and awaken a nation. True revival always begins when God's people return to his revealed truth. When Scripture is neglected, worship becomes routine; when rediscovered, repentance follows. Churches today must guard against losing the Book in the house of the Lord—forgetting the authority of the very word we claim to proclaim. God still transforms hearts through the faithful reading and hearing of Scripture. Reform begins wherever the Bible is opened, read, and obeyed.

2. Repentance is more than regret

When Josiah heard the law, he didn't explain, excuse, or delegate blame—he tore his clothes and humbled his heart. Genuine repentance involves both sorrow for sin and action that restores obedience. Josiah didn't just feel conviction; he led change. True repentance accepts God's verdict and moves toward renewal. Like him, believers must measure repentance not by emotion but by transformation. The tender heart God honors is the one that hears his word and obeys it without delay. The same humility that spared Josiah's generation still opens mercy's door for ours. When Scripture exposes sin, repentance should not wait for comfort—it begins the moment conviction comes.

3. Faithful leadership inspires covenant renewal

Josiah's faith was contagious. He didn't reform Judah by decree but by example—standing by the pillar, reading Scripture aloud, and vowing to follow God "with all his heart and all his soul." Faithful leaders do not command repentance; they embody it. In the church, families, and communities, renewal spreads when those in authority model obedience authentically. Influence flows from integrity. Like Josiah, Christians lead best when their devotion is public, consistent, and grounded in God's word. Every generation needs leaders who love truth enough to confront error and hope enough to call others back. When leadership bows before Scripture, God's people rise in faith.

4. Reform without renewal cannot last

Josiah's reforms were bold and thorough, yet after his death the nation returned to sin. Outward change without inward conversion fades quickly. Laws can restrain sin, but only love for God can remove it. The story warns that external success—clean temples, national unity, visible zeal—cannot substitute for transformed hearts. True faith survives not because a godly leader commands it but because God's Spirit sustains it. Every believer must move beyond admiration for Josiah to imitation of his devotion. The same word that changed a nation must continue to change each heart daily. Without inward renewal, every revival becomes a moment rather than a movement.

CONCLUSION

Josiah's reign shines as the final bright flame before Judah's exile. The book that was lost was found; the word once forgotten shaped a nation again. His story reminds believers that revival is not born from emotion or power but from hearing and obeying God's truth. Yet even Josiah's zeal could not erase generations of rebellion. The law could reform hearts for a moment, but only grace can renew them forever.

As the curtain closes on Judah's independence, the next chapter will bring Babylon's invasion and the fulfillment of long-ignored warnings. Yet the God who preserved his word in Josiah's day would preserve his promise in exile. His truth cannot be buried; it always rises again.

REFLECTION

1. What does Josiah's discovery of the book of the law reveal about spiritual neglect?
2. How did Josiah respond when confronted by God's word?
3. What role did Huldah's prophecy play in shaping Josiah's reform?
4. Why did Josiah's covenant renewal begin with public reading of Scripture?
5. How did Josiah's destruction of idols fulfill God's earlier promises and warnings?
6. What does Josiah's death teach about the limits of human-led revival?

DISCUSSION

1. How can churches today rediscover the power and centrality of God's word?
2. What distinguishes true repentance from mere regret or emotional reaction?
3. In what ways can spiritual leaders model obedience that inspires renewal?
4. Why do outward reforms often fail to produce lasting spiritual change?
5. What can we learn from Josiah's humility and "tender heart" toward Scripture?
6. How can believers guard against letting God's word become neglected or forgotten?

12

THE FALL OF JUDAH

2 KINGS 23:31-25:30

Objective: To show that sin brings judgment, yet God's mercy endures and preserves hope beyond exile.

INTRODUCTION

In 79 AD, the Roman city of Pompeii vanished beneath volcanic ash. Life ended in a moment, yet archaeologists later discovered that destruction came after years of warning tremors. The mountain had spoken; the people ignored it. Judgment rarely falls without mercy's prior voice.

Judah's fall followed the same pattern. After Josiah's reform, four kings ruled—each weaker, more fearful, and more rebellious than the last. Egypt claimed tribute, Babylon invaded, and prophets pleaded in vain. The nation that once carried God's covenant now resisted his commands. Walls fell, the temple burned, and Jerusalem's survivors marched into exile. Yet even amid ruin, the story does not end in silence. God's promise to David still flickered in the darkness, preserved in the release of a forgotten king.

In 2 Kings 23:31–25:30, we witness both the collapse of a nation and the persistence of divine grace. The God who judged Judah did not abandon his covenant. Exile is not the end of the story—it is the field where hope takes root again.

This lesson explores the consequences of rebellion, the certainty of God's word, and the mercy that still shines through the ashes of judgment.

EXAMINATION

Kings in decline (23:31–24:7)

The final chapters of Kings unfold like a slow funeral procession—the crown of David passed from one unfaithful ruler to another until it fell into foreign hands.

Jehoahaz, son of Josiah, reigned only three months before Pharaoh Neco removed him and imposed heavy tribute on Judah. Egypt again became Judah's master. The son of a godly king quickly forgot his father's reforms; righteousness, it seems, is not hereditary. Jeremiah lamented Jehoahaz as "a young lion captured in a pit" (Jer. 22:10–12). His exile to Egypt fulfilled God's word and began Judah's submission to foreign powers.

Pharaoh replaced Jehoahaz with his brother Jehoiakim, renaming him to mark his new allegiance. He reigned eleven years—longer in length than in faith. Jehoiakim taxed the people to pay Egypt's demands (23:35) and later rebelled against Babylon after Nebuchadnezzar defeated Neco at Carchemish (605 BC). His rebellion was both political and spiritual; the narrator declares, "Surely this came upon Judah at the command of the Lord, to remove them out of his sight, for the sins of Manasseh" (24:3).

Jehoiakim embodies the futility of resistance without repentance. He fought enemies abroad while ignoring sin at home. Jeremiah portrays him as arrogant, self-indulgent, and murderous (Jer. 22:13–19). His death passed without mourning, fulfilling Jeremiah's prophecy: "He shall be buried with the burial of a donkey."

Kings in exile (24:8–25:21)

Jehoiakim's son Jehoiachin inherited a throne already trembling. He was eighteen years old and reigned only three months before surrendering to Nebuchadnezzar (597 BC). Babylon's second invasion stripped Jerusalem of its treasures, its leaders, and its future. "He carried away all Jerusalem… only the poorest people of the land were left" (24:14). The exile began.

This is the theological point of no return for Judah. The curse of Deuteronomy 28 had arrived: the people were uprooted, the temple was plundered, and the king was humiliated. Yet even in this catastrophe, God's sovereignty is clear. Babylon was not acting freely; it fulfilled the word of the Lord spoken through the prophets.

Nebuchadnezzar appointed Zedekiah, Jehoiachin's uncle, as puppet king. His reign lasted eleven years—long enough to prove that human defiance cannot overturn divine judgment. Despite Jeremiah's warnings to submit peacefully, Zedekiah rebelled again. Nebuchadnezzar responded with an 18-month siege, cutting off food until "there was no bread for the people" (25:3). When the wall was breached, the king fled but was captured on the plains of Jericho.

The scene that follows is one of the darkest in Scripture: Zedekiah's sons were slaughtered before his eyes, and then his eyes were put out. The last sight he saw was the death of his legacy. Zedekiah became the living symbol of Judah—blind, bound, and led into exile.

In 586 BC, the inevitable arrived. The temple, palace, and walls of Jerusalem were burned; sacred vessels were carried away; priests and officers were executed at Riblah. Nebuzaradan, commander of the guard, ensured that nothing remained of Judah's glory. The writer's tone is painfully restrained—as if words themselves bow under the weight of divine wrath.

This destruction is more than a political tragedy—it is a covenant consequence. Every warning of Deuteronomy came true: disobedience had produced exile. The land that once flowed with milk and honey now lay desolate. This was the un-creation of Israel. The temple, once God's dwelling, was dismantled like the tabernacle of Eden after Adam's sin.

The kingdom of Judah died, but not without meaning. The same God who tore down its walls would one day rebuild its hope. For now, silence settled where praise once rose.

Remnant and mercy (25:22–30)

After Jerusalem's destruction, a small remnant remained. Nebuchadnezzar appoints Gedaliah son of Ahikam as governor over the poor who were left in the land. His appointment fulfilled Jeremiah's counsel to "seek the welfare of the city" (Jer. 29:7). For a moment, it appeared that peace and restoration might still be possible. Gedaliah encouraged the survivors: "Do not be afraid... serve the king of Babylon, and it shall be well with you" (v. 24).

But even this fragile stability collapsed. Ishmael, a descendant of David, assassinated Gedaliah out of nationalist zeal (v. 25). The killing of the governor—the one man entrusted with rebuilding—shattered any remaining order. Fear spread, and the remnant fled to Egypt, reversing the Exodus and repeating old mistakes. The final act of Judah's history was another flight into slavery. The people who once sang of freedom now returned to the land of bondage.

The book could have ended there—in silence and despair—but it doesn't. In a surprising epilogue, hope flickeed once more. Decades later, during the reign of Evil-Merodach of Babylon, Jehoiachin, the exiled king, was released from prison. He was given royal clothing, a seat of honor at the Babylonian table, and a daily allowance "all the days of his life" (vv. 27–30).

This closing scene is a whisper of resurrection. The Davidic line survived; the promise endured. Though the temple was gone and the land lay in ruins, God's covenant thread remained unbroken. The open-ended conclusion invited readers to look forward—to exile, to return, and ultimately to the Messiah who would restore the throne forever. Even in Babylon, mercy sat beside judgment. The story of exile became the soil from which redemption would grow.

APPLICATION

1. Sin always finishes what it starts

Judah's fall did not happen overnight. It was the slow harvest of generations that refused repentance. From Manasseh's idolatry to Zedekiah's pride, sin matured until judgment became unavoidable. Scripture warns that unconfessed sin never remains contained—it always spreads, corrodes, and consumes. God's patience is long, but it is not endless. The fire that finally consumed Jerusalem had smoldered for centuries. For believers, the lesson is urgent: every small rebellion is a seed of ruin. Confession uproots what delay allows to grow. When the heart resists correction, history repeats its fall.

2. God's word stands when everything else falls

Every promise and warning spoken by the prophets came true. The temple burned, the kings were exiled, and the land lay desolate—just as God had said. Judgment fulfilled is proof that his word cannot fail. Yet that same word also preserved hope: the release of Jehoiachin testified that covenant grace still stood. Scripture's reliability cuts both ways—it assures both consequences and compassion. The Bible is not a collection of idle words; it is life and truth. Christians must build on its certainty, trusting that what God declares, he will accomplish—whether in discipline or deliverance.

3. Human power cannot replace spiritual faithfulness

Judah's kings tried diplomacy, rebellion, and alliance, but none could substitute for obedience. Jehoiakim's arrogance, Zedekiah's cowardice, and the remnant's fear all prove that strategy without surrender fails. God does not bless self-reliance; he honors trust. The kingdom's end teaches that strength apart from righteousness is only weakness delayed. Today, churches and nations fall into the same trap when they rely on influence instead of integrity. Faithfulness remains the true defense of God's people. Obedience may seem small compared to armies or wealth, but it alone invites divine protection. The fall of Judah declares that rebellion ruins faster than wisdom can rebuild.

4. Grace survives even in exile

The last image of Kings—a captive king freed and fed in Babylon—proves that grace survives judgment. God's promises may pass through fire, but they never burn away. The release of Jehoiachin is not nostalgia; it is a preview of redemption. Even when God's people lose land, temple, and crown, they do not lose him. Christians find the same truth in the cross: wrath spent, mercy revealed. No failure is final where faith endures. The exile ended not in silence but in supper—the king eating daily at the table of mercy. Hope remained, even in Babylon.

CONCLUSION

The book of Kings ends where rebellion always leads—ashes and exile. Yet within judgment's darkness, grace still flickered. Jehoiachin's release in Babylon was more than history's footnote; it was God's quiet reminder that his covenant would not die in captivity. The throne of David remained reserved for a greater King who will rule forever.

Judah's story closes, but God's story continues. The same word that judged also preserves, proving that divine mercy always outlasts human failure. Exile may remove the people from the land, but it cannot remove them from God's plan. Through ruin and restoration, Kings teaches one lasting truth: the Lord is faithful even when His people are not.

REFLECTION

1. What patterns of disobedience led to Judah's downfall?
2. How did Jehoiakim's and Zedekiah's choices reveal rebellion against God's word?
3. Why was Jerusalem's destruction more than a political tragedy?
4. What does Gedaliah's assassination show about Judah's spiritual condition?
5. How does Jehoiachin's release at the end reveal God's mercy?
6. In what ways did the exile fulfill both God's justice and his promise?

DISCUSSION

1. What warning does Judah's slow collapse offer to believers and churches today?
2. How can we guard against spiritual drift before it leads to disaster?
3. Why does trusting God's word give hope even in times of judgment?
4. What modern examples show the danger of relying on power instead of faithfulness?
5. How does Jehoiachin's restoration illustrate the endurance of God's grace?
6. What can exile—and God's mercy within it—teach us about repentance and renewal?

www.ingramcontent.com/pod-product-compliance
Lightning Source LLC
Chambersburg PA
CBHW060341050426
42449CB00011B/2808